ON THE LEVEL

(A BRICKIES TALE)

David Bruce

authorHOUSE®

AuthorHouse™ UK Ltd.
500 Avebury Boulevard
Central Milton Keynes, MK9 2BE
www.authorhouse.co.uk
Phone: 08001974150

First published by AuthorHouse 11/24/2008

ISBN: 978-1-4389-1255-4 (sc)
ISBN: 978-1-4389-1262-2 (hc)

Printed in the United States of America
Bloomington, Indiana

This book is printed on acid-free paper.

This book is dedicated to Scott 15.10.1960 – 10.1.2007. A loving husband, a devoted father, and my best mate!

FORWORD

My name is David Bruce. I am a bricklayer by trade. All my friends call me 'Minty', a name that I was unfortunately saddled with as an apprentice, after the only two occasions I was late for work. It baffled me for a few weeks as to why everyone was calling me 'Minty', but eventually someone at work explained it to me. 'Minty', after eight, get it? No, I didn't but the name stuck, and now nearly some thirty years later I am still known by that name!

I apologise in advance to all the people I have mentioned in this book. They will all know exactly who they are but I have taken the liberty of changing their names in a vain attempt to protect the guilty!

I began writing this trilogy of books while my wife and I were living in Andalucía, in a small white washed village in the mountains of Spain. It all began after making one simple phone call to Scott, my best mate, who was at the time still living in South Africa with his wife and nine kids! I called and unfortunately got the answer-phone. Slightly annoyed at this, I left a rather rude message as Scott and I had not spoken to each other for quite some time. A few days went by and I received a call from Malcolm, Scott's father, who very, very sadly told me that Scott had been killed in a road accident involving his beloved

V.W camper and a rather large lorry! After the shock of Scott's death began slowly to sink in, I sat reminiscing over the last thirty years I had known Scott and about the times he and I had spent together both socially, and also in our work environment. I couldn't believe he was gone forever, and a few days later I made the decision as a tribute to Scott, his beautiful wife and children, to put pen to paper, to share with you the ups and downs, the laughter and tears and all the crazy, crazy things that had happened to us over the last thirty years of travelling the world making a living as bricklayers.

I hope you enjoy reading this book, as much as I have enjoyed bringing Scott back to life as I best remember him!

I APPRENTICE

For those of you who have been unfortunate enough to have gone through an apprenticeship, you will without a doubt understand exactly how I felt. Always the youngest, always the butt of very, very cruel jokes and always doing the shitty jobs that no one else wanted to do. Without fail always the scape goat for anything and everything that happened to go wrong, Regardless of who was actually responsible for it! I was often mentally and also without doubt physically abused by all the older bricklayers. Each and every one of them took great pleasure in causing me as much embarrassment and discontent as they possibly could. They would spend hours and hours each day dreaming up new ways in which to make each and every day as hard as possible for me! Regular tricks would be nailing my work boots or clothes to the walls or floors with six inch nails. They would urinate of defecate into my tool kit when my back was turned. Throw my tools in all directions, let the tyres down on my motorbike, put horse manure into my sandwich box (or worse!), and shove fibre glass insulation down the back of my trousers as I was bending over working. Nail gun me to a wall or a tree and leave me there helpless for hours on end! Then my pet hate, being made to empty the chemical toilet out, 'yuck.' In fact, they did anything to make me react, which was exactly what they wanted, the more I reacted the worse the pranks became.

I worked for a small building company that mainly specialised in agricultural buildings, which often meant the use of the bricklayers' nightmare, "the nine inch concrete block." They are extremely heavy and even heavier when wet! Their edges are always razor sharp and cut your fingers to shreds. My tormentors at work insisted I had to lay these monster blocks all day long, six or seven courses high! Just so they could see my face going a deep shade of purple struggling with the effort, I was not going to be beaten not by these bloody idiots!

My employer 'Alan' was also a life long member of the sadists society, and also took great pleasure in assisting the rest of the gang in dreaming up daily, new and impossible tasks for me to perform. As a snotty nosed kid, because that is all I was at the time, I was told to, and more often as not screamed at until I complied with their requests and demands no matter how stupid or impossible they seemed.

This torture, because that is exactly what it was, began at seven thirty in the morning and continued relentlessly all day long until four thirty in the afternoon, Monday to Friday but excluding Wednesdays. As Wednesday was my day release at college, and god was it a release from these bloody animals at work, but this Wednesday was going to be different, very, very, very different indeed.

It was mid nineteen eighty one and Scott and I found ourselves standing there at college clutching a piece of paper each in our grubby little hands. Scott and I had buddied up at the beginning of college some four years previously and had remained inseparable ever since! The certificate we now held in our hands gave us the grand title of 'bricklayers'. God was I chuffed, and I thought to myself now it was going to be payback time, my time! I was going to get myself an apprentice!

As we walked out of the college for the very last time we decided to retire to the pub to celebrate, and as Scott's father owned the White Horse public house, it was off to the White Horse that we went. In fact it was very handy because Malcolm, Scott's dad spent from six a.m. until he fell over sometime p.m. extremely Jonnie Walkered up! So he never actually noticed that Scott and I never, ever paid for a pint and I'm sure he still has no idea even to this day! (Sorry Malc). Needless to say, we celebrated all afternoon and rather too well as it happens, but that's exactly what they invented Stella for, isn't it? And babbling and dribbling in the corner decided together the following morning to cruise all the local building sites, with our new licences to make money and find ourselves a job as 'bricklayers'. An hour or so and some five pints later, I poodled off home on my motorbike, as by now poodling was all I was capable of. On returning home I told my mother the good news, to which her reply was "Oh that's nice dear," and then she promptly added without taking breath that the house keeping money I was paying her would now increase accordingly! I should have kept my stupid, big gob shut!

The following morning I met up with Scott at the White Horse, and nursing the mother of all hangovers, we slowly trundled from building site to building site, and eventually by two p.m. landed ourselves a job at the princely sum of £52 a day! Wow, how good is that I thought, as I had only been earning just £26 a week as an apprentice! I had just increased my earnings by a massive ten fold. I was about to become absolutely loaded! We left the site with what can only be described as a stupid grin on our faces.

II PROPER JOB

Visits to the pub which had previously been impossible on our apprentice's wages, unless of course, we went to the White Horse, gradually increased from just two nights a week, to Thursday nights, Friday nights, Saturday nights and Sunday afternoons after football. I had never in my life had so much money, and I started to spend it almost as fast as I was earning it. Three weeks after qualifying, my girlfriend was complaining bitterly that she never saw me anymore, never knew where I was and was totally sick of going from pub to pub in a vain attempt to locate me. When eventually she did find me she was sick of all my mates taking the piss out of her. She had had enough of it, and what exactly was I going to do about it? I was only twenty years old, what was I going to do about it? Absolutely nothing, I was having far too much fun with my new found wealth!

I had met Carol at Richmond Ice Rink, some three years previously, a place where we use to hang out once or twice a week, and over the years Scott and I had by trial and error developed and honed to absolute perfection a great way of meeting new girls! It went something like this; skate around the rink until you find a pretty girl, who is obviously having a bit of trouble standing up on her skates. Once you have located your prey, skate around in the opposite direction, keeping an eye on your target. Then when the opportunity arises, skate into her head on, knock her flat on her back, apologise profusely, cop a quick grope if you can and then pick her up literally and by way of an apology offer to take her for a drink in the bar! The success rate was approximately eighty to twenty. Not bad odds really and I had, over the years managed to meet a lot of girls this way, Carol included and because she was quite local to me, we had become an item. Was this relationship going to last I hear you say? To which the answer was a resounding NO! I was now single again as I hunted around my bedroom, trying to find where I had hidden the bloody alarm clock the previous night to ensure it would wake me from the Stella haze that always followed the Sunday after football. Eventually I found it stuffed in a drawer, switched the bloody thing off and looked out of the window.

God, how I hated the dark wet mornings, but now as winter was slowly approaching, the dark, wet and freezing cold mornings were even worse, especially when you are riding a motorbike, which by the way for those of you that may be interested was a lime green Kawasaki KH 250, my little baby. The only downside of riding a motorbike is when it's cold, you freeze to death, and I always found myself stopping to warm my hands on the engine at least two or three times on the way to work. This particular Monday was extremely cold, and as I left the house I decided that the bike would have to go! I had passed my car driving test some three years previously, care of my parents giving me driving lessons as a birthday present. Little did I know as I started my bike, that this day could quite easily have been my last day!

As I pulled away, cursing the cold weather, I noticed black ice on the road, and also a light fall of powdery snow but nonetheless, off I went. Scott and I had arranged to meet in a small café, just two minutes from the building site for coffee and bacon sarnies. It was a ritual we had performed every morning for the past seven months. It also gave me half an hour or so to thaw out sufficiently and regain blood circulation in my hands and feet!

The building site was in Maidenhead, which meant me going across country to get there. I had been using the same route for over seven months and I knew it like the back of my hand. I was running a bit late, so I was speeding a bit, maybe 70mph-ish, but my face was beginning to burn with the cold, even wrapped up with a scarf and a balaclava, I was absolutely bloody freezing. I slowed down a bit in an attempt to warm up a bit. As I did so in front of me I saw a huge lorry lumbering down the road and a short distance in front of the lorry coming towards me a small feeble light, which I presumed was a moped or pushbike or something. Mirror, signal, manoeuvre, I hear you say? Nope, I dropped it a cog and gave it a handful of throttle. As I started to pass the lorry at some 70 or 80mph, I saw exactly what this feeble little light was. It was an old Morris minor, with the offside front light out, and it was only 10m in front of me. *Shiiiit!*

7

I hit and bounced off the roof of the old Morris minor, after having nearly totally removed my wedding tackle on the petrol cap of my motorbike, and as I flew through the air I found it surprising as to what went through my head. Not, have I or will I break anything, or god this is bloody going to hurt, but shit, I bet that is going to bend my brand new stabila level! Weird or what? Touchdown was almost fortunate, as I had missed the hard asphalt road completely, but I landed face down in a drainage ditch full of barbed wire, glass and other prickly things. I was winded and lay there gasping for breath, and not being able to move was worrying the hell out of me! Suddenly I heard this voice above me, "are you hurt son?" What do you think you stupid old fart. I retorted, and then I asked him if my bike and brand new level were ok. The old man replied that my bike was fine, apart from the fact that it was buried halfway into the bonnet of his car! Ironic, isn't it that just that very morning I had decided to buy a car.

III TIME OUT

A compound knee fracture a broken collar bone two broken wrists, five broken ribs and six fingers. My face and chest looked as if someone had been using an orbital sander on me! At the hospital, mum and dad were going into total meltdown about the dangers of riding motorbikes and how could I have been so stupid as to hit a car head on! I was getting a new lecture every two minutes or so about the benefits of four wheeled transport and how lucky I was no to be dead.

At last the doctors pinned and screwed my knee back together, set and plastered my wrists and nearly six hours later told me I could go home, but I must return twice a week to see a doctor and monitor my recovery.

Oh, deep, deep joy. I was now a prisoner at home. I could not walk, I looked like an advert for platex-bras with this stupid shoulder brace I was wearing for my broken collar bone, which thrust my chest out and my shoulders back. I couldn't cough, laugh, sneeze or even fart without pain shooting in every direction in my body. I could live with that no problem because the most embarrassing part of my predicament was, with two broken wrists my mother, of all people, was having to wipe my bum! Try to picture that one?

Scott came around the following night after work and we spent a few hours talking about the crash, the pain, and the fact that there was absolutely no way that I would be able to go down the pub until such time as the potty training became a one man operation again. My life was on hold until I was mended again, bollocks, and double bollocks!

The video player was a new fangled piece of kit in nineteen eighty one, and was also horribly, horribly expensive. So needless to say we didn't have one. So as the weeks slowly dragged on I had to make do with watching every black and white Johnny Weissmuller Tarzan film, every Elvis film, every spaghetti western film ever made in dispersed with Tom and Jerry, Mary Mungo and Midge and the Clangers! Daytime T.V was absolutely soul destroying, but in between this mind numbing experience, I was visiting my hospital for regular check ups and eventually some physiotherapy on my broken knee. My wrists had now at last healed, so after nearly eight weeks I was mobile again, sort of, with my new crutches. But the best of all, I was at last independent in the toilet again. *Hallelujah!* Being mobile with my new crutches was quite good fun, but as my physiotherapist (Jane) walked into the room, the first thing she said to me was, "we will have you walking again without those in three to four weeks." It still hurt to put any weight on my left leg. I was absolutely going to hate this, but I know I wasn't because Jane was twenty four years old, blonde, and she had a body that could stop a clock! I knew this because I could see her skimpy underwear through her tight white uniform.

I started to look forward to physio on Mondays and Thursdays, apart from the fact that she was a sadistic bitch and made me walk the treadmill for forty minutes at a time without supporting myself. My left leg muscle has wasted away to nearly half its normal size, and looked more like it belonged to a chicken and not to me. According to the x-rays and Jane, the work the doctors had done on my knees was superb and I only needed more exercise to be able to walk properly again. So the treadmill became the tool of torture for the next few weeks, after which time Jane suggested we went to the swimming pool to further my recovery by using water resistance. I wasn't listening at all; I was imagining what this beautiful blonde girl was going to look like semi-naked in a bikini! Alas, I was very, very disappointed indeed. She stood at the side of the pool, barking orders at me like a sergeant major. My illusion had been completely and utterly blown out of the water.

That night Scott came round and I had my first excursion to the pub for over two months. It was bliss Stella, still tasted like Stella, and yes you've guessed it, I got completely bladdered. We sat in the snug with the fire roaring, talking, laughing and drinking, at last my life seemed to be back on track.

IV AFRICA

I went to watch Scott play football on the Sunday and after the game sitting in the pub, Scott dropped the bombshell. "I've been offered a job," he said, "in Africa; the money is fantastic, nearly £500 a week and its tax free." "What's the catch?" I asked. "A two year contract," he said, "I've had the interview and I'm off this coming Thursday. I was gob smacked because I'd known Scott nearly five years and was honestly quite annoyed he hadn't mentioned it to me in the past." And what the hell am I going to do," I blurted out, "we work together, we're mates, I don't want to work on my own or with some idiot I don't even know, and what's Jackie had to say about all this?" Jackie was Scott's long suffering girlfriend of nearly six years, and according to Scott, as soon as she had finished college she would go out to Africa and join him. "Brilliant," I said sarcastically.

Thursday came and we all went off to the airport to see Scott off. Malcolm, for the first time ever I think, was almost sober; Mary, Scott's mother just cried continually and Jackie was throwing the biggest wobbly I think I've ever seen. I said my goodbyes to Scott, and left him to deal with the nuclear explosion that was about to occur at the entrance to departures.

I was watching football Saturday afternoon, when the phone rang.

It was Scott, he was very excited and I was having a job to understand what he was saying as he was talking so fast. Eventually he slowed down to a pace where he became coherent again. "Its fantastic here," he said, "I'm staying in a small hotel, quite near to where I'll be working and it's only costing £4.50 a night with breakfast included. The weather is great, I've met my new boss, and I start work on Wednesday. They've given me a few days to relax and find my bearings." All of a sudden I became very jealous of him, and I told him so. "Don't worry," he said, "get yourself over here when you're back on your feet, they love the English here. You'll get a job with me no problem." He left me the hotel phone number and I promised to call him on the Friday night.

We spoke once or twice a week for the next four or five weeks until my dad received the quarterly phone bill and threatened to remove a certain part of my anatomy with something blunt and very rusty. Scott continued to call on Friday nights, but this particular Friday he didn't call. The next day worried, I called his hotel, and the woman who answered said he had checked out on the Tuesday just gone. I thought he must have found a more permanent place to live or maybe somewhere nearer to where he was working.

I had my last physio appointment the following Monday, and eventually plucked up the courage to ask Jane out for a drink. I was a bit surprised when she agreed, and also said she would come and pick me up. Oh joy, things were looking better all the time. I got back home to find Jackie waiting for me, she wasn't looking very happy at all, and as I got out of the car she ran over to me and began to cry. "What ever is the matter?" I asked her. Malcolm had apparently not heard from Scott either, and as Jackie and Mary were in pieces with worry, he had made a number of phone calls including one to the company that Scott was working for. And after speaking to the company director, had managed to find out that Scott had not only filled in the application for his job, but being only twenty one and not worldly wise, had stupidly applied for citizenship. The downside was that he was now a citizen and became instantly eligible for army service and had been dragged off to do a two year stint in the army! Jackie was beside herself. It looked to me like Jane was going to have to wait. Jackie wept and wailed for nearly two hours solidly and nothing I did or said would console her. She didn't want to go inside, she didn't want a cup of tea, she didn't want a cigarette, she didn't want anything apart from Scott, and she wanted him right now! We were still standing in my parents' driveway when Jane pulled up in her car. She saw the tearful Jackie, put two and two together, or so she thought, and disappeared up the road as fast as her little fiesta would carry her. This was going to take an awful lot of explaining I thought, but that would have to wait until Jackie was back on an even keel! Meanwhile, Malcolm was making slow progress with the Embassy in Africa, and was trying to find the British consulate, with a view of getting the idiot son of his, hopefully off the hook and back home as soon as possible to face the music.

Scott had received a letter at his hotel, some two weeks previously, saying he must attend the local police station to register. He had complied with the letter and trotted off to what he thought was a mere formality for newly arrived immigrants. On arriving he had filled in the registration, only then to be told he must go to another address which the officer had given him for yet another interview! Scott obliged, jumped into a taxi and off he went to the next interview, which turned out to be a very extensive medical. The penny hadn't dropped yet; Scott was still labouring under the false impression that this was normal procedure that was until he was given a uniform and told to report for duty!! Unbeknown to Scott, Angola was now on the cards.

Any work that Malcolm and his family had done and also the British consulate had proven to be absolutely futile. Scott was in the army and that was where he was going to stay. He began his basic training and after a few weeks was issued with a rifle. Scott phoned me out of the blue and said although he was very frightened about what had happened, he was also, in a strange way quite enjoying it, and had at last been able to call home to explain his predicament to his family. "What are you going to do now?" I asked him. Not a lot was the answer, "I'm here now for two years like it or not!" We chatted for another five minutes or so, and he said he would send me his address so we could at least write to one another. I hung up the phone; poor bastard I thought.

I was now at last back to work and had actually bought a car, with money that I had managed to borrow from Dad. Borrowing money from Dad had its pros and cons. Sometimes he forgot completely that he had lent me any money at all and other times he was continually on my back demanding impossible payments every five minutes. Luckily for me this was one of those times when he forgot, well almost anyway.

My new car was a 1974 Mark III Cortina Coupe 2.0L, hardly boy racer material I hear you say, but it got me to work and I quite liked being mobile and independent again. I had paid £399.00 for the car, but the only problem it was the sickliest orange you have ever seen, but it was mine and I loved it.

I was now working with a Welsh brickie called Darren; he was quite a good trowel but he had this habit of whistling a tuneless whistle all day long which drove me and everyone else on site up the wall. I was missing working with my mate Scott and I was thinking of moving on to another site and another sub-contractor, but on that Friday night I had a nice surprise. My wages had gone up to £58 a day and I was now earning nearly £300 a week. I decided to stay put for a while.

That evening I told my mother the good news and to my absolute horror, she insisted I now paid her even more housekeeping. A very valuable lesson had just been learned and I never again mentioned to her about any wage increases that I received.

Scott called that evening and after a very brief chat he explained as he was only earning the equivalent of £200 a month, he felt obliged to use his money to phone Jackie, as it is so expensive to call home. I said I understood and as he was not able to receive incoming calls, we said we would keep in touch via letter. I didn't speak to Scott again for nearly nine weeks.

I had a letter from the tax office; I ripped it open and inside was a cheque. I had a rebate for £402.00, fantastic I though. "What's that?" asked my father. "A tax rebate," I replied. He looked over my shoulder and snatched the cheque out of my hand. "Mine," he said. "What do you mean?" I asked. "You owe me £400 for your car, this will cover it." "Not fair" I replied, but it was too late for any argument, I knew I had lost before I had begun.

It was now mid May and the summer was in the air. I love this time of year, it has always, as long as I can remember, been my favourite time of year, with everything coming into bloom, and smelling so nice, not too hot as to make you uncomfortable at work, but still warm enough to sit in the beer gardens of pubs in the evenings without freezing yourself to death.

After about a million and ten phone calls and a lot of grovelling, Jane had at last condescended to meet me for a drink and soup in a basket at the shoulder of Mutton in Mattingly. On the way home she jumped all over me, and we cemented our friendship in a small car park by Black Bush airport.

The world according to me was now all roses. I had a really good job and I was also earning very good money. I had transport of sorts, and now the most important attribute of all, a girlfriend. Lovely, things could not be better. The weeks were flying by and all of a sudden it was July! As I got home from work, the phone was ringing. I picked it up; it was Scott. "Come pick me up please," he said. "Where are you?" I said. "Dover," he replied. "Bloody hell, I'll be there in two hours," I said. He sounded absolutely awful. I scribbled a quick note to my Mum and jumped in the car. In the end it took me nearly three hours to get there, the traffic was bumper to bumper all the way. At last I arrived in Dover, it took me over an hour to locate Scott and when I eventually found him, I hardly recognised him. He had lost about three stone and his clothes were hanging off him. He looked gaunt and tired. We did the man hug thing and I asked him where his bags were. "What bags?" he replied.

As he fell into the car I noticed he was limping rather badly, and I asked him what he had done to his leg. As we drove home, Scott began his story. Four weeks into his basic training, he had been doing live round target practice, with the rest of the new recruits and he was lying in the prone position, shooting at targets some three or four hundred metres away. A shot rang out; another recruit still had a live round in his rifle and was standing behind Scott. The bullet had entered Scott's thigh and exited just below his groin. Scott was rushed into hospital and operated on to stop the bleeding and to treat the shock.

He had remained in the hospital for almost four weeks, and eventually became mobile again. As soon as he was able he had grabbed his passport and what little money he had managed to save, and did a runner, with only £400 he had hitched lifts with lorry drivers, taken buses and had even walked for days at a time, until he got another lift or found a bus or train to take him a bit further on his homeward journey. Eventually, and I must say with an awful lot of luck considering how volatile Africa is, he had managed to make it to North Africa. It had taken him nearly four weeks to get there. He got a boat to Spain and managed to beg some money from the British Embassy to get him through Spain and eventually into France by train, and from Calais he had got the ferry to Dover and that was it, he said. "Bloody hell Scott you've gone absent without leave," I said. "Yes," he mumbled, and promptly fell asleep.

I headed for the White Horse as fast as I could, with the windows open because Scott stunk like a skunk. I even considered stopping and getting some deodorant for him to dull the overpowering pungent aroma, but I though it better to get him home as quickly as I could.

It was after ten thirty when I pulled into the White Horse car park, and through the windows I could see Malcolm lumbering up and down the bar. He was an ox of a man, almost as wide as he was tall. I charged into the pub and ran up to Malcolm babbling almost incoherently. "Hello David," he said, "Stella is it?" "No, no, no, I've got Scott in the car outside." He sobered up almost instantly and began shouting to Mary who was in the kitchen. By this time Scott had woken up and had walked into the pub. I knew this for one reason and one reason only, which was I could smell him!

Mary screamed and Malcolm ran to his boy, if you can call it running that is, something similar anyway and bear hugged him to the point of nearly breaking every bone in Scott's body. "Christ you stink," he said, then suddenly without any warning dissolved into a flood of tears. Mary was still fighting her way through the crowd of regulars, still screaming Scott's name, and Jackie who was working behind the bar promptly fainted on the floor!

Needless to say I never made it to work the following morning, as Malcolm had declared the drinks were now on the house, which was nothing new to Scott or me! But we stayed, as did most of the regulars, drinking and celebrating Scott's return to after five in the morning. Jackie never stopped grinning all night, and between her and Mary, spent all night clucking over Scott.

Breakfast was a right royal affair, and Scott by now had had a shower and was no longer peeling the paint off the wall, or making peoples' eyes water with the smell. Scott sat there solidly eating for over two hours. I was glad to have my best mate back home, and happy he was back where he belonged.

V NEW START

I noticed there had been a few internal changes to the White Horse since I had last been there, and I asked Malcolm what he was doing. He said they were knocking the two bars together in order to make more room for the restaurant area, and moving a few internal walls to make new toilets, in an attempt to attract more customers.

Over the next few weeks, Scott recuperated at home after his ordeal and the White Horse became a regular haunt for me again. Scott had been helping the builders to build the odd wall here and there, and had suggested to the foreman that maybe we could do some weekend work for them. A week later we had weekend work and as much as we wanted. Three weeks later we were offered a full time job and I jumped ship to start work full time in the pub renovation business.

This kind of work was great, you always got a free meal from the publicans and because they wanted the pubs to be finished as quickly as possible so they didn't loose too much trade, we found our selves, more often as not, still working late into the nights, and as we were paid hourly it meant we were earning very good money.

This particular night we were breaking out the old ramp they used to roll the beer barrels down into the cellar on, which was made of wood and concrete. The chippies were due in the morning, so we had to finish it that night. We heard last orders being called at the bar and were still breaking out the last remaining pieces of concrete at just after eleven p.m. The skip was nearly full and all we had to do now was to get the rest of the rubble out of the cellar, and we could go home.

Unbeknown to us, the concrete breaker had set off a vibration alarm in the bank next to the pub, and the next thing we knew, the whole place was swarming with police, who did not give Scott or I the chance to explain exactly what we were doing in the cellar. They just assumed we were somehow trying to break into the bank through the cellar wall, and arrested us on the spot.

Guildford police station is a soulless place and the cells quite cold! We had two or three interviews in the few hours that followed and eventually some bright spark had the common sense to phone the landlord of the pub and check to see with him that what we were saying was the truth.

At last we collected our personal effects from the desk sergeant, thanked him for their hospitality and entertainment and drove back to the pub. It was now after 3.30a.m. The breakers were gone and so were most of our tools. "Bloody brilliant," said Scott. We closed the cellar door and drove home very annoyed indeed. The next day we arrived at the pub and Des, the landlord could not stop laughing for over an hour, but bless him, he had picked up our tools and the breakers and locked them up in his garage, so all was not lost.

Another great perk of working on the pubs was the fact that any demolition work often produced slate roof tiles, bricks, floor boards and other items, which we took straight to the re-claim yards in the area. This sometimes provided enough money for the occasional session down the pub!

1983 arrived, and January was extremely cold but the good thing about pub work was, we never lost any time with bad weather because we were normally inside, and therefore not affected by the frost or rain. This also reflected in the amount of money we could earn, and as I was still living at home with my parents, it was time for a new car.

I drove to the nearest Ford dealer in my now very dirty and slightly battered Mark III and part exchanged it against a brand new XR3i. Now this was typical boy racer material. It went like the proverbial off a shovel. The dealer told me to bring it back at fifteen hundred miles for a free service. The following week I arrived back for the service, the salesman was gob smacked. In the last week we had terrorised every pub from the New Forest to Watford and back, I loved this car, it was great! The only downside was the local constabulary must have liked it too because they were always stopping me to get a better look at it, and give me a few points into the bargain!

In a very short time, I had accumulated six points on my license. Time to calm down I thought, well maybe anyway. The XR centre at Byfleet was a great place to spend my hard earned cash on new wheels, tyres, new high performance exhaust systems, and also some engine modifications. I spent the next few weeks spending an absolute fortune on my car, and now this little car was quick, very quick indeed, in fact, so quick the Speedo needle was going almost around to the needle stop, the rev limit had been removed and the mechanic had told me under no circumstances to exceed 7.5 thousand RPM, or face the consequences.

I wanted to know how fast this little car of mine was capable of going. Steve, another good friend of ours, was in the motorway division of the police force, and drove a police prepared XR4i with a tachometer. I called him and we arranged for him to follow me in his XR4i to see exactly how fast I was going.

We had agreed to meet him on the stretch of the M25 between the M3 and the A3 and as we were going ten pin bowling at Tolworth it would be on the way.

Sure enough he was parked on the hard shoulder, exactly where he said he would be. We drove past him at a speed that nearly took his doors off. On came the blue light. Nice touch I thought, I waited for him to catch up and then floored it, we were weaving in and out of the 3 lanes, the Speedo needle went past the 140 mark and carried on. Steve was still right behind me, lights flashing, I was going absolutely flat out.

Eventually we slowed down and I turned onto the A3 and then

onto the hard shoulder The XR4i pulled in, in front of us and stopped. The door opened and this huge gorilla of a man got out, *oh shiiiit!* It wasn't Steve! "Where's the fire Stirling?" he said, "we clocked you at 146MPH, this is going to cost you son," he added. It did cost me big time, they threw the book at me in court, banned me for a year and fined me for reckless driving, failure to stop and also having engine modifications without informing my insurers. I had only had my little car for 3 months. Not fair. Scott's V.W camper became the new works bus and my car was destined to stay in the drive!

Jane called and invited me to her parent's house for a meal, which I thought quite odd because her parents had taken an instant dislike to me from the day I had met them. Anyway I got changed, grabbed a taxi and dutifully arrived half an hour later, with a bottle of wine and some flowers for her mother.

Jane's father was a surgeon and had apparently been offered a post at a specialist hospital in New York. He had accepted the post and had arranged to rent their house out. They were going to be leaving in ten days time. Good, I thought, peace and quiet at last. But then he added, "Jane is also going to be coming with us because I've managed to get her a senior position in the physio department of the same hospital. So ten days later I was technically single again, although we had promised to wait for each other. Yeah right.

I had no car or no girlfriend but I did have my freedom again to go and do boy stuff again, without being nagged to death for doing it. I took full advantage of my situation and spent the next few months being a pain in the arse to all and sundry!

Scott announced that both he and Jackie were going on holiday the following week, to Holland on a cycling holiday, and would be back in two weeks time. As my parents were by now totally fed up of being my personal taxi service, running me here, there and everywhere, I also had no option but to take a holiday as well.

I dug out my fishing gear, and spent the next couple of weeks carp fishing. It was great, I had not been fishing for nearly a year and I promised myself I would not let it be so long next time.

VI NOORDWIJKERHOUT

Scott and Jackie returned the following Saturday and we all met up for a drink in the White Horse. Scott had that stupid look on his face that I had come to recognise over the years that I had known him, and meant he was going to say something that he though was of mind blowing importance. "You two have gone and got yourselves married," I said before he could open his mouth. "Don't be bloody stupid," he replied and then added, "I've found us a job in Holland, in a small town called Noordwijkerhout, where we've just been on holiday. The money is brilliant, the accommodation is free and the wages are paid weekly straight into your bank account.

We moved onto a corner table in the pub and went over and over again; the job, the pay, and the location. Scott's mum Mary had seen us plotting in the corner and came over to find out exactly what we were up to! Before Scott could manage to get two sentences out of his mouth, Mary had slammed her fist on the table and began ranting on about the last little adventure in Africa, there was absolutely no way Scott or I for that matter, was going to go!

Bastiaan, a Dutch guy met us at the Hook of Holland port in a small café. We had just spent the best part of 3 hours in customs with Scott's V.W camper. As at the time both Scott and I had long hair, I think they must have thought we were smuggling counterfeit clogs into Holland or something!

Bastiaan's English was almost accent free, we had a quick cup of coffee, and then followed Bastiaan down the road in his beat up old land rover, and he was flying along. Scott was having a job keeping up with him in the camper. I was looking out the window. We were driving on the top of a dyke, and below some 4 or 5 metres both to the left and right were the houses. It was weird looking down into the properties.

"Where the hell has he gone now?" said Scott. "Four or five cars in front," I replied. "Can I overtake?" said Scott, and pulled over a bit. "No!" I screamed, as a huge lorry just narrowly missed the front of the V.W.

After nearly ten minutes we eventually managed to catch up with Bastiaan's land rover but just as we did, the lights and bell began flashing and ringing on a railway crossing. We had to stop. Bastiaan had seen us and pulled over to wait the other side of the barrier.

"Fag break," Scott announced. So we sat there smoking and waiting for the train to pass. Two rather pretty blonde girls on horses walked past us and stopped in front of the barrier, also waiting for the train to go by. Not two minutes later along came an old man with two Jack Russell's and a shopping basket and stood next to the two horses. The two dogs instantly began sniffing at the horses' feet. The horses were becoming more and more agitated by the dogs. One of the girls on the horses turned to the old man, and obviously said something quite rude in Dutch to him about his dogs. The old man took a dim view to the out burst, and probably the language as well. He then tied the two dogs to the barrier and turned to the two girls, waving his walking stick and shouting.

The argument was just getting properly going when the train suddenly thundered past at such a speed it had made me jump. The lights stopped flashing; the bell stopped ringing and up went the barrier, dogs and all.

We could not move we just sat there laughing and laughing. I had never seen anything quite so funny in all my life; Scott was crying with laughter. The girls reached up and untied the dogs and passed them back down to the old man, who by this time had gone into total meltdown.

We eventually managed to proceed and Bastiaan was off again at break neck speed, Scott and I right behind him. We followed him for nearly another hour until Bastiaan suddenly indicated left and we followed suit down a bumpy dirt track until at last we had reached our destination.

"Oh my god," I said, "what the hell is this place?" a ten foot high chain link fence stretched into the horizon, both left and right it was topped with razor wire and halogen lights! The main entrance had a double barrier system and a small wooden hut, outside were two security guards patrolling up and down. We had arrived at what looked something from the Great Escape film. "Bloody hell," said Scott, "what have we let ourselves in for here then!" "*POW* camp," I said.

Bastiaan waved to us and we got out of the camper, and followed him into the security building. They took our pictures against a blank wall and five minutes later gave us a laminated card, each with all our details on; occupation, employers' name, nationality and the expiry date of our contract, which was six months. Bastiaan told us we needed these passes to move from area to area within the site and also to get in and out of the site. "Don't lose them," he added, "or you'll be stuck."

The site itself was absolutely massive. It was going to be a huge shopping and sports complex, with living accommodation and also a marina. In total there were eight cranes of which two were mobile, crawling up and down on train tracks, dropping materials left, right and centre.

On the left hand side of the main entrance were hundreds of porta-cabins. Some were offices for the architects, some for management, and others for storage. But most of them, as I had expected, were the accommodation blocks. They were stacked three high and stretched along the fence for nearly 400metres.

As we followed Bastiaan down the track it became very muddy about five to six inches deep, the camper was struggling to get through the muck and as it was mid-summer and quite warm, in fact it was over twenty six degrees Celsius, I was perplexed to see so much mud.

Scott pulled over next to Bastiaan and we got out of the camper, stepping carefully onto wooden pallets, so we didn't disappear up to our ankles in mud. Bastiaan explained because it was so hot, the concrete they were pouring for the new floors was going off too quickly and they had to spray it with water, to stop it drying too quickly and cracking. Hence, the reason there was mud as far as you could see.

We followed him into the cabins, wondering what exactly we were going to find. It was actually, believe it or not, quite nice and not anything like the horror stories I had previously heard about from other bricklayers that had done the same thing. The bedrooms were very small, about six by eight feet, with a rudimentary bed and side cabinet, and a small wooden wardrobe. At least I noted it had a lock on the door! From the sleeping area you walked down a passage way into a large area, maybe 8m by 8m square. This was the canteen and social area. Next room along was the kitchen and directly behind that was the showers, toilets, and washing machines.

Bastiaan said it was all Englishmen in this particular unit, and it was time to go and meet the other bricklayers and our new foreman. We followed him like little sheep in and out of the buildings, until eventually we came across the rest of the bricklayers, all beavering away.

"David!" shouted someone; I turned around to see who it was. Oh god I didn't need this, I didn't need this at all. It was Alan, my old boss from my apprenticeship days. I hadn't seen him for nearly three years and was hoping I would never bump into him ever again. "What are you doing here, son?" he asked. "The same as you," I replied, "laying bricks for loads of money," and then I added, "what's the foreman here like?" "You're looking at him," replied Alan.

My heart sank as the memories of the cruelty this man had caused me in the past came flooding back to me. "Who's this long streak of piss?" he said, indicating Scott. "This is Scott, my best mate," I replied. Scott is 6'4 inches tall and looks like a cross between a flagpole and a preying mantis, because he is so long limbed and quite skinny. "Oh," said Alan, "right, grab your tools and follow me, you pair of wankers." And so, it began again.

As we followed Alan, I turned to Scott and said, "We are going to have to nip this in the bud now, or this idiot is going to have us jumping through hoops before the end of the week." Scott agreed. We rounded a corner and walked slap bang into the rest of Alan's motley crew. This was about to become a bigger nightmare than I had first imagined!

Hey David, you gay bastard, this your new boyfriend, then rang out. I recognised the voice instantly; it was Ray, the worst of the pranksters. The rest of the gang erupted into fits of laughter. I walked up to Ray and said, "One more remark like that and you'll be wearing that level around your neck, you prick." "Oooh," said Ray, "Fancy your chances?" and burst out laughing. "I'm not your little play thing anymore," I replied, "I'm not here to fetch and carry for you lot anymore, I'm not an apprentice, I'm a bricklayer now." Roars of laughter again erupted.

Damian walked up to me and said "hello David, nice to see you again. How's things been going?" "They were going fine," I said, "up until about half an hour ago." "Don't worry," he said, "they'll get bored and leave you alone in a day or two." "I hope so," I replied.

Now Damian was the only member of Alan's crew that I actually had any time for, a very kind and quiet man. A born again Christian, and not really the type you would expect to find working as a bricklayer on a building site. He would cringe when people swore, and chastise you if you upset him by using the 'F' word, saying you would pay the price for your blasphemy when the time came. He was mid-forties, single and spent all of his free time at the church, or making model aeroplanes. No wonder he had never married, and still lived at home with his mother. Apart from that I knew he would be an ally against the tormentors, as he had been when I was an apprentice.

We went to work; we had missed the morning shift but still had six hours to go before knocking off time. Alan found Scott and me a large manhole to build. It was obviously one that nobody else had wanted to tackle, and he left us to it. The working day began at seven a.m. and finished at 6 p.m., with two half hour breaks, one at 10.30 and the next at 2.30.

Two thirty rolled round fairly quickly and Scott and I walked back toward our container. Although we had a kitchen in the unit, the Dutch had laid on a catering service which consisted of mobile burger vans, of which ten or twelve were scattered all around the site. We chose the nearest one. The menu was in Dutch, and the food was also mostly Dutch. Raw fish, seafood platters cheese flavoured sausages, the odd burger and chips, and everything came absolutely smothered in mayonnaise.

Bastiaan walked up behind us, "Everything ok lads?" he said. "Yes," we replied simultaneously. "Try the raw herring," he said, "it's lovely." He picked up a whole herring without its head, tipped his head back and dropped it down his throat. "Lovely," he said, and handed one to both Scott and I. Not to be outdone, I followed suit, tipped back my head and dropped the small fish down my throat. Ten seconds later, up it came again. Scott and Bastiaan were still laughing when I eventually managed to stop coughing and start breathing again. "I think I'll have a burger," said Scott, "me too," I said.

The rest of the day was fairly uneventful, and at 6 o'clock we walked back to the lock up, put our tools away and then back to our new lodgings, only to find that our nightmare was going to continue. Alan and his crew were our new companions in our unit. Oh shit, we quickly showered and went outside to find a burger van and got something to eat. We ordered yet another burger and coke, and sat in the warm evening sun contemplating our fate.

There was a complete alcohol ban on the site, although you could drink within the confines of the living areas, so we ordered a few beers and sat until the sun disappeared over the horizon. As luck would have it, there were three pay phones on the site and I though I had better call home to stop my mother sending out a search and rescue party to retrieve me. Scott came along as he wanted to call Jackie and his family. Anyway we stood in the queue for over half and hour before we eventually got our turn. My mothered answered on the first ring. "Hello dear, everything alright?" she asked. "Yes, thanks mum," I said and then I told her Alan, my old boss and his crew were also on the job. "How lovely," she said, "at least there's someone there you know." If only she knew, I thought. I promised to call her on the weekend and hung up.

The following morning I awoke with a start, to the sound of running water. I sat bolt upright and looked around, the floor was covered with over two inches of water and I could see a hose pipe dangling over the top of my door! I jumped out of bed and tried to salvage my clothes, which were soaking wet, along with my wallet and passport, which by now was almost totally illegible. Scott came flying around the corner; he had also received the same treatment. He was fuming mad, we found some dry clothes and went down to the burger van for coffee and something to eat. The rest of the mental retards were standing there almost crying with laughter. "I suppose you think that's funny," I said to Alan, and as I said it, Scott ran past me and landed a punch straight on Alan's nose. It all went off, arms, legs, fists, ashtrays, chairs; everything went flying. The man in the burger van slammed the shutter down, shouting some abuse in Dutch as he did so. Needless to say, Scott and I were hopelessly out numbered at eleven to two so we, very soon, found ourselves on the floor, nursing a black eye and a fat lip. Then Ray turned to Scott and said "you hit like a stupid girl Scott," and bang, off it went again. But this time, we got a little more than we bargained for, and found ourselves locked in the toilet block for two hours to cool off or so Alan had said.

Thankfully the rest of the week was quite uneventful, apart from the odd verbal insult or two, and nothing really nasty happened at all. Friday morning arrived; we had breakfast and headed off for work. An hour later we were on our way back. The silo system which had provided the mortar had broken down and Bastiaan sent us home with pay. Scott and I thought after showering, to go and visit the local town. Noordwijkerhout, as the diet of burgers we had eaten, had made Scott constipated and we needed to find a chemist to remedy the problem. I stuck my head into the social area and asked if anyone needed anything from the chemist. Ray shouted, "Extra large condoms!" and again the room fell into uncontrollable laughter. Alan walked up to me and said, "Can you get me some suntan cream, factor twenty, as I'm starting to burn quite badly." He did actually look like a lobster with a great mop of ginger hair hanging out the top!

Scott and I walked up to the camper, which hadn't moved since Monday and we jumped in. Scott turned the ignition key; the engine turned and turned but wouldn't start. All of a sudden this huge backfire sounded and the camper fired up. The idiots had rammed two potatoes up the exhausts, as we pulled away they were all hanging out of the windows roaring with laughter. As we drove down the road some two or three kilometres later, the VW began kicking out great clouds of black smoke behind us. The idiots had also squirted oil up the exhaust pipes!

We parked in Noordwijkehout right next to the town hall and explored our new environment. The town itself was typically Dutch, and everything centred on the town hall and radiated out from this central point. We found a map on a bus shelter wall, made this our focal point and spent the best part of the day exploring the small side streets in every direction. In the lower level of the town next to a canal, was a market square, which was full of locals buying and selling local produce including livestock, cheese, vegetables, flowers, even wooden toys, tools and electrical goods. It was a fascinating place, we left the market and stumbled on a chemist almost by accident and went inside.

Scott explained to the chemist what his problem was which somewhat embarrassed him, and she showed him two or three different products to choose from. He was adamant he didn't want the suppositories and I can't say I blamed him, which left just the tablets. They looked more like sweets than medicine and came loose in a paper bag. A plot began to hatch in my head, and I told Scott to buy some more. He looked at me quizzically. "I'll explain later," I said. I grabbed a bottle of the highest factor sun cream I could find and also a bottle of baby oil.

We left the chemist and Scott said, "What in gods name are you up to?" I simply said one word to him, "Revenge." We stopped in a small restaurant, had a few beers and also our first decent meal in nearly a week, which was lovely and not a burger in sight! As we drove back towards the site, I began to explain my plan to Scott. By the time we arrived back at the site, we knew exactly what we were going to do!

I emptied about 80% of the suntan cream down the sink and replaced it with baby oil. I cleaned and shook the bottle and we both walked into the social room. I gave the bottle of suntan cream to Alan; he just grunted something and carried on watching some rubbish on TV. Scott walked around offering 'sweets' to everyone, and being greedy sods they were, they ate the lot!

We retired outside for yet more beers, and to await results, some two hours later after nothing had happened; we went back inside to watch a bit of television. Not fifteen minutes after we came back in,

Ray suddenly jumped up and rushed off in the direction of the toilets. I looked at Scott, he was grinning like a Cheshire cat, then without warning, up jumped Paul and shot off in the same direction. There were only four toilets in the shower block and before long all the traps were full, Scott and I were trying not to laugh out loud, and so it went on, one in, one out, one in, one out. Alan went down to the burger van and actually accused the poor guy that he had poisoned everyone with his cooking. This didn't go down too well, and the guy told him, he and his crew were no longer welcome to eat at his van anymore! Scott and I sat and watched the musical chairs for the next two or three hours, before we at last got bored and went to bed. I lay there wishing tomorrow was Monday, so we could see the results of Alan's suntan cream.

Saturday arrived and we went out in the camper to have a proper look around, but we didn't get far. The backfire caused by the potatoes had caused the exhaust manifold to split, so we spent all day, and over two hundred pounds getting it fixed at a VW dealer in Noordwijkerhout. On our return to the site the lads had not been out all day and were complaining of stomach cramps and diarrhoea. I felt so sorry for them. Not.

We got up early Sunday morning, and as the catering service was only operational from Monday to Saturday, we decided to go out early and find ourselves breakfast somewhere. As luck would have it, not more than six kilometres up the road was a small hotel. We drove in and parked up, looked at the menu on the wall, which was also written in English and German, found full English breakfast written halfway down the menu and charged in, salivating at the thought of something normal to eat.

I had heard the saying, 'never trust a skinny cook,' and the woman who met us inside and took us to our table was far from skinny and dressed in her kitchen whites. Looked more like a Mr. Whippy ice cream, sort of thin at the top and progressively bigger the further down you went! We ordered our breakfasts and she disappeared into the kitchen. The hotel was fairly small, and full of wood from floor to ceiling, very clean, and I noticed on the wall it was only twenty eight guilders a night, about £10 for a room. Scott said it would be ideal for Jackie if she came over for a long weekend. The waiter came out with the coffee and to our surprise it was Bastiaan. "What are you doing here?" I asked him. "Good morning," he said, "This is my family's own hotel, you must have met my wife, Stella already, she's the cook!" He then added, "We're all going canal jumping today, would you two care to come along after you've had your breakfast?" We both agreed as it sounded like a lot of fun.

Stella returned with our breakfasts, and I was trying to imagine this huge woman being able to get up enough momentum to actually launch herself across a canal! We finished our food and then followed

Bastiaan and Stella down the road in the camper. less than ten minutes later we pulled off the road into a field, full of beer tents and stalls selling various types of food and drinks

The canal jumping was already underway and we watched as different competitors ran with a long wooden pole, similar to pole vaulting poles, but not quite as long, towards the canal as fast as they could. Then the pole was thrust into the canal, and hopefully with a bit of luck, over you went. The opposite side of the canal had been laid with 150mm of sand, to facilitate a soft landing, and also, once raked flat, showed the distance each competitor had achieved.

We stood and watched, beers in hand for maybe half an hour, as the various competitors, some dressed in traditional Dutch costume, others in crazy colourful suits with top hats, and one completely naked, went charging towards the canal. Bastiaan said, "Would we like to have a go?" Scott and I jumped at the chance, paid our entry fees, pinned our numbers to our shirts and followed Bastiaan to choose our poles. Bastiaan went first, to show us his technique and promptly ended up in the canal, which was full of foul smelling water and thick mud. The crowd were roaring with laughter. Scott, the long shank went next, and how he managed it I will never know, went straight into the lead on his first attempt with a jump of over 8m, jammy bugger. I went next and only just managed to clear the canal by the skin of my teeth. The five shortest jumps from each round were eliminated from the competition, and apart from Bastiaan, Scott and I went through to the next round. I managed three more rounds before I ended up in the canal, stinking and covered in chickweed. Scott went one better and got into the fifth round, before he also came to a sticky end. As all three of us were now muddy and smelly, we retired to the beer tent, and spend the rest of the afternoon drinking and chatting with Bastiaan and Stella.

At eight in the evening, we said our goodbyes and thanked both of them for an exceptional day and made our way back to the site. We stunk to high heaven, and on our arrival headed straight for the showers to freshen up. We also thought it might be a good idea to wash our stinking clothes, so we got some washing powder from the vending machine on the wall, and explored the knobs and dials on the washing machines. It was going to be trial and error as all the instructions were in Dutch! We selected a high temperature, chucked in the powder and hit the start button.

The burger van was now our only sanctuary from abuse, so we went outside for a smoke and a few more beers. The evening was very still and warm, and before we knew it, it was dark. We said goodnight to the burger guy and went back inside to retrieve our washing. But on entering the washroom, we noticed both the doors of the washing machines were open and on the floor were three empty green bottles. I knew exactly what was in these bottles as I could smell it. Bleach!

The sods had opened the top loaders and poured the bleach into each machine. I could already see the damage it had caused to my clothes. We put more washing powder in and repeated the wash cycle again.

That was it, WAR was now declared, we had only been there for one week, but that was the last straw. These arseholes were going to pay and pay big time! Monday morning, I met Scott at the burger van for coffee and croissants; we still had over two packets of laxative pills left, so round two went into operation.

We picked up our tools from the lock up and off to work we went. The sun was already hot and by nine o'clock I could see Alan smothering his suntan cream on his face and arms. Two or three of the other lads were also using Alan's cream. I looked at Scott, he was grinning from ear to ear. Scott went into action and started offering 'sweets' around, and as before the greedy sods ate the lot!

Justice had at last been served; all we had to do now was to wait for the results. This time was somewhat quicker than the last and before long, Alan, Ray, Dave and also Paul had gone rushing off towards the nearest toilets. We were beginning to enjoy our revenge but the best was yet to come.

As Alan and his crew had been banned from our burger van, Scott and I had time to talk at breakfast time without being continually bombarded with insults from the idiots, who were now eating at the next van down from us.

"Shall we tell them what we've done?" said Scott. "Not a good idea," I said, "We may need to do it again at a later stage, and it may also save us getting a kicking." So we agreed to keep quiet. By now it was in the high twenties and gradually getting warmer by the second, and by midday it was well over thirty degrees Celsius. The air was hot and still, which was making everyone sweat like crazy. We were drinking litres of water and at 2.30 had to go to three or more burger vans before we managed to find one that hadn't run out of water or coke.

That afternoon Alan moved me and Scott to an area that was full in the sun, while he and Ray continued with the wall we had been building, as it was now in a shaded area. We could see them giggling behind the wall thinking that had pulled a good one, but both Scott and I enjoy the sun and as we tan quickly and only very rarely burn, this didn't represent a problem to us at all. The afternoon soon passed and after showering, we yet again sat outside by the burger van sipping a few bees and having a smoke.

We could hear a commotion in the unit and went in to see what was causing all the noise. On entering the social area, we saw Alan lying on a bench on his stomach, still in his shorts, howling in pain, and Ray was standing over him and was trying to lance a blister about 8 inches in diameter on his back. It was full of water and looked extremely painful. I hoped it hurt like hell!

"You want to rub some yoghurt into that," said Scott, "It will take the pain away and help to ease your sunburn." "Piss off, you Pratt," replied Alan. "Only trying to help," said Scott. I noticed both John and Paul also had their share of painful looking blisters on their backs and arms too. Ray's head looked as if it was about to explode, it was a deep shade of red and his eyes were also swollen quite badly. As he was almost totally bald, the top of his head had received the most damage and was erupting in small white and red blisters all over the place.

Scott motioned to me that we should go back outside, and we made sure that we were far enough away as not to be heard, and broke down into fits of laughter. We strolled past the payphones and as they were completely empty we thought we would call home quickly. I got my parents answer phone and left a short message. Scott was on the phone for ages, so I went back and ordered two beers and waited for him to return. He came back nearly half an hour later and I knew something was wrong as soon as I saw his face. "What's wrong?" I said. "Jackie's pregnant," he said with a big stupid grin on his face. "Do you know who the father is?" I replied jokingly. We ordered enough beers to float a small ship and sat at the burger van celebrating fatherhood into the early hours of the morning. Tiredness eventually caught up with us and we stumbled off to bed.

I unlocked my bedroom door only to find the bed upside down, the mattress had been slashed with a knife, the wardrobe and side cabinet were in pieces, strewn across the floor and my clothes scattered everywhere. "They've done the same to me," said Scott as he walked into my room behind me. "How the hell did the buggers get into our rooms?" I said. Scott tried his key in my door lock and it clicked open, "Like that," he said. Was this really self-inflicted, I asked myself, or is it just that Alan and the others were just complete arseholes. We tidied up our trashed rooms and half an hour later went to bed.

The rest of the week was incident free because Alan and the rest of the Muppets were wallowing in self pity as their blisters began to burst and in some cases get infected? It was very satisfying to see them suffering this way, but also incredibly hard to keep from laughing out loud.

Thursday night we walked up to the payphones only to find that some retard had decided to vandalise them and steal the money, so we had to drive up the road to find a payphone. I spoke briefly to my parents, and Scott called Jackie. She had booked a flight and was coming over the following evening for the weekend. We rushed off panicking to Bastiaan's hotel and booked a double and a single room for Friday and Saturday night. Once everything was sorted, we sat with Bastiaan and Stella drinking and chatting.

Bastiaan said he had noticed that we were getting a lot of aggravation from the rest of the gang and asked us what was causing it. I told Bastiaan I had worked for Alan as an apprentice and it was almost a tradition in England for the apprentice to get most of the tricks and gags played on them. But as we were still the youngest, I supposed they thought it was fair game to continue playing these stupid games at our expense.

Bastiaan sympathised with us and then he added, "If it gets out of hand, please let me know." We thanked him for his concern, and made our way back to the camper. We hadn't gone more than four hundred metres when the offside front wheel came off. We went flying off the road, across the tram tracks, which ran parallel to the road, and smack, into a concrete post which supported the electrical overhead cables for the trams. Neither of us had seat belts on, the steering wheel stopped Scott, but I went straight through the windscreen. I remembered this flying through the air sensation from my last accident, but the landing this time, thankfully, was a lot softer. Scott jumped out the window as his door would not open. "You ok?" he asked. "Yeah, I think so," I replied. I had lost my two front teeth, my head hurt like hell, and my cheekbone was killing me. Scott had a huge bruise forming on his forehead and was complaining that his ribs were hurting.

By this time there were two trams, one either side of the camper, waiting but unable to pass because the camper was blocking their path. Bastiaan appeared from nowhere, and said an ambulance was on its way. We both began complaining but he would not have any of it.

At the hospital, they pulled the small pieces of glass from my forehead, and stitched up the 4 inch gash in my cheek, and a dentist made me some temporary teeth and told me to return in a few weeks time to get my new permanent caps. Scott had broken three ribs, and had a huge bruise the size of an egg on his forehead, but apart from that he was unscathed. The kept us in overnight and discharged us at 9.30 the following morning. Bastiaan, bless him, was already waiting for us, and drove us back to his hotel, where Stella fussed over us all day long, making drinks, sandwiches and anything else she could think of, to try and make us feel better.

The camper had been towed back into the hotel car park; we went out to survey the damage. It was without a doubt a complete write off. The front had been pushed back over two feet and neither of the front doors would open. The sliding door was buckled, most of the glass had broken and the roof had a big crease in it. I could see that Scott was upset. The camper was his first vehicle but it was also his pride and joy. He had bought it from a pensioner some five years previously and even now it had only covered twenty six thousand miles. "You know they're without a doubt responsible for this," said Scott. "I don't think even they would stoop so low," I replied but I knew that he was right.

We took a taxi to the airport and met Jackie at just after eight o'clock. 'You two been fighting again' was the first thing she said to Scott as she walked up and hugged him. "No," we replied simultaneously, and Scott recounted the events to date that had happened to us in the taxi on the way back to the hotel. "Right," said Jackie when Scott had eventually finished, "Take me there right this minute and I'll sort them out myself." "Don't bother," said Scott, "We can deal with anything they throw at us." We stayed at the hotel bar that night.

The following morning at breakfast, we introduced Jackie to Stella. They got on like a house on fire, and Stella said there were some push bikes in the garage if we wanted to use them, but to make sure we locked them up if we left them anywhere.

We finished our breakfasts and went out and opened the garage. We pulled out three push bikes, and the only way to describe them, is to say they looked like 1950's postmen bikes with only one gear, and they weighed an absolute ton each! Cycling was Jackie and Scott's hobby, so they didn't give a hoot. A bike was a bike and off we went.

The cycle paths in Holland are brilliant and run parallel to all the main roads so there's no way you can get lost. We headed for Noordwijkerhout some ten kilometres away. With the wind in our faces it was very hard going and the bikes were so heavy which didn't help. The biggest insult was small kids on bikes half the size of ours, were flying past us at twice our speed but we persevered and nearly 40 minutes later we arrived in Noordwijkerhout and we chained and locked the bikes to an iron bridge.

I thought I would leave the love birds alone for a while and said I would meet them back at the Blue Tulip pub next to the bridge at 4 o'clock for some food. We parted company and I wandered around the shops and bought myself some new gloves for work, as the blocks at work were beginning to cut my hands to pieces. I also got half a dozen new t-shirts to replace the ones damaged by the bleach. Twenty minutes later I was bored of shopping and headed back to the Blue Tulip. It was only just twelve o'clock. I ordered a hertogjan beer, my favourite Dutch beer and a tuna salad and sat watching the world go by.

I had been there no more than ten minutes when a very pretty blonde girl just plonked herself down beside me and said, "Hi, my name's Shelly." "You're a kiwi," I replied. "No, I'm Australian," she said rather indignantly. "I'm David," I said. "You're Irish," she replied. "Nope, English," I said and we both laughed. Shelly was an air hostess, who on her free time came to Holland to visit her brother who worked in Holland as a cooper making oak barrels. By the time Jackie and Scott arrived, nearly 4 hours later, both Shelly and I were quite well pissed and getting on like a house on fire. We all had a meal together and spent the rest of the evening drinking until the early hours of the morning. As we left, Shelly said she would pop up in the morning in her brother's car and show us around the area.

We peddled off towards the hotel, wobbling all over the place but at least this time we had the wind behind us, thank god, and managed to get back home in just over half an hour. I awoke Sunday morning and immediately wished I hadn't. I had one of those hangovers which only hit you on one side of the head, just above my right eye. My head hurt like a bitch. I stumbled down for breakfast, feeling very, very delicate indeed.

No sign of Scott or Jackie, but Shelly was already there drinking a cup of coffee. "You look like death warmed up," she said. I mumbled something almost incomprehensible and dropped like a stone into the seat next to her. Stella came crashing out of the kitchen. The door banged against the wall, it felt like it was banging against my head. She took one look at me and disappeared into the kitchen, yet again slamming the door in the process. Two seconds later, the door crashed open again. In came Stella with a huge jug of coffee and a packet of aspirin. "You look awful," she said. "Thanks," I managed to croak. "Drink all of this coffee and take two of these," she said, thrusting the aspirins into my hand, and five minutes later she bought out my breakfast. It took me ages to plough my way through it but after I had finished, I felt almost back in the land of the living.

"Self-inflicted," said Shelly suddenly, making me nearly jump out of my skin, "I've got no sympathy for you or your condition at all." "Thanks," I mumbled. Jackie came in and announced that Scott was trying to get out of bed with a hangover and was feeling very sorry for himself. "My god," said Shelly, "All you Poms must be like girls, can't drink to save your lives," and began laughing.

Scott staggered in five minutes later looking like he had been dragged through a hedge backwards, and said, "Coffee, just give me coffee," and collapsed into a chair. Two pints of coffee and a breakfast later he was nearly functioning again, so we jumped into Shelly's car and off we went. Shelly took us to a quite large town called Leiden, which had all the benefits that Noordwijerhout didn't. It had huge shopping centres, sport arenas, bowling alleys and every other thing you could possibly need. In fact, the town itself was infectious. The more you saw of it, the more you wanted to see. We walked around for hours and hours and eventually knackered, found a rather nice restaurant next to a canal, where we sat watching the huge barges and boats chugging up and down, eating and drinking as we did so.

Jackie's flight home was at 4.00 so sadly we had to cut the afternoon short, so we could get her back to the airport. Scott insisted that he would take Jackie to the airport by taxi and leave me and Shelly to have a bit of time together at the hotel. We arranged to meet outside the building site at 5.00. The taxi arrived; Jackie gave me a hug and said "Look after Scott for me," and was gone!

"Well," I said to Shelly, "When are you next back in Holland?" "About two week's time," she replied. "You can get a message to me here at the hotel if you want?" I said and left it at that. It was soon time to get going, so I paid Stella for the rooms and the drinks, and Shelly drove me back to the hell hole! We sat in the car for nearly half an hour talking and just as I was about to get my tongue down her throat, Scott started banging on the window. He was jumping up and down like demented monkey. I opened the window, "What's up?" I said. "They've gone, they've gone," was all he could say. "Who's gone?" I asked. "Alan and the gang you idiot, that's who!" Now I was out of the car and we were both jumping up and down like lunatics. Shelly drove off without warning, hooted once and was gone. "Now look what you've done, you Muppet," I said, "And I haven't even got her number." "Oh well, never mind," said Scott. "Thanks," I said, and with that we walked back through security to our cabins. Inside looked like a bomb had gone off. There was junk everywhere, clothes, tools, suitcases, newspapers, and half eaten food scattered all over the floors. On opening my bedroom door, I found they had also left me a fair well present, which was stinking in the middle of my bed. "Animals," said Scott, holding his nose. We chucked all the rubbish in the skips outside but it wasn't until I cleaned my room that I found a note stuffed under my pillow. I called Scott and read it to him. It was from Damian.

Dear David, Scott,

I'm sorry about all the terrible things that the boys have been doing to you. Had I known they were going to do something so dangerous to your camper I would have told you I do hope you are both alright. Bastiaan told us about the accident Friday and sacked us all on the spot. Please phone me if at all possible to let me know you are ok.

Best Regards,
Damian

A number then followed. "Told you, told you," said Scott, "I knew it was them, the bastards." "Well it's over now," I said. "Yeah but what about my camper?" he said, "I'll never find one like that again, it was mint, not a mark on it, perfect inside..." He ranted on for another five minutes, before he ran out of expletives and finally calmed down.

Monday morning before work, Bastiaan found us having coffee and told us to meet him in his office at 7.00, we dutifully complied. He gave Scott the accident report from the local police, which Stella had also translated into English for us, bless her, and said you will need this for your insurance company. Scott thanked him and Bastiaan also said if you need to use the telephone, use this one in my office. "Thank you," again said Scott. "I'm putting you two with a German gang today," said Bastiaan and off we went with him to find them. The Germans stopped work and came up to Bas. He rattled off something in German, and one by one they walked up to Scott and I, shook our hands and said good morning. There were all dressed the same, white trousers, white vests, short hair and most of them also had a moustache. It made me and Scott look out of place with our army combats, dirty t-shirts and hair halfway down our backs!

The foreman, Andreas, found Scott and I a wall to build, and so the day began. We watched the Germans working, they were very clean, very precise but bloody hell were they slow. By the time two of them had laid two courses, Scott and I had finished our wall and were looking for another to start. They almost seemed to work in formation and when breakfast time came, they even seemed to eat in unison. But their burger van was ten times better than ours was. They had everything. Twenty seven different kinds of sausages, obviously burgers, they had salamis, pickles and also fruit, which were great. The only downside was everything came absolutely smothered in a curry or chilli sauce, but we were spoilt for choice, and made pigs of ourselves. This was great; at least we had a slightly better diet to look forward too. Plus of course, the best of all we had no Alan and the crew to make everyday a misery. The days began to fly past and we were both actually starting to enjoy working in Holland at last.

Scott's insurance company called and made him an offer for the camper. He turned it down flat and he then told them to try and replace the vehicle in that condition and mileage for the money they had offered. So began the wrangle for his money with the insurance company.

We needed transport, we were starting to feel like prisoners in the site and walking up to the payphone was taking over an hour in each direction. We asked Bastiaan if it was possible for him to pay us cash for a few weeks so we could buy a car. He said, "No problem," and then said, "Stella's selling her VW golf, would you like to have a look at it?" That evening Scott and I went for a quick spin in the golf and decided to buy it. Bastiaan said we could pay for it weekly, so he stopped £200 a week from our wages until it was paid for. We paid £600 for the car and £90 to insure it. We were mobile again at last.

"I think you've got a VW fetish," I said to Scott, he just grinned at me. We had a few drinks with Stella and Bas and then drove back to the building site. On our arrival we found the social area full of suitcases, tools, and ten English blokes, milling around, all with cans of beer in their hands. We introduced ourselves and were instantly bombarded with a million questions. 'What's it like here, where is the nearest pub, where's the phone, who's in charge, when do you get paid, what time do you finish work, where's the toilet, and where's my mum?'

There were all chippies from Newbury in their late twenties and early thirties. At least we had some English to chat with at last. Scott and I continued to work with the German gang, and the days began to blend into one another. It was nearly the end of August and boiling hot, over thirty degrees Celsius. Bastiaan turned up and gave me a piece of paper; it was a message from Shelly. She was coming to Holland that Friday and would pick me up at 7.00 Friday rolled round and after work I jumped in the shower, washed all the important nooks and crannies. I even brushed my hair and showered. I walked up to the main entrance, she was already there, she gave me a quick peck, admired my new teeth, and the now purple scar on my cheek.

"Where are we going?" I asked. "I want you to meet my brother Peter, you can stay at his house tonight if you want to," she added,

"Then we can hit the town!" "Ok," I said, "Sounds good." We arrived at a beautiful 3 storey town house some twenty minutes later. "This is Peter's house," said Shelly as she opened the door, and there on the doorstep was Peter. He towered over my by at least 4 inches, maybe 6'7 inches. He was obviously a body builder and he had arms like my legs! I put my hand out and said, "Hi, I'm David, nice to meet you." He shook my hand and said, "You hurt my baby sister and I will kill you! Ooops I though but I knew he really meant it.

We had a fantastic evening in parts of the town I'd never seen before and eventually we staggered home at after 3am. Shelly showed me to my room, said goodnight and disappeared into hers. I was itching to sneak into her room for a cuddle (if you like) but this image of Peter bursting into the room and catching my deflowering his sister and bludgeoning me to death with something heavy and blunt kept popping into my head, so I decided to stay put in my room!

I woke with a start, as Shelly was jumping up and down on my bed. "Get up, get up, we're going fishing with Peter." Now this was my idea of a good day out. I was up dressed and ready to go in five minutes. We drove no more than five minutes down the road and into a trout farm, got a rod and a day permit and went fishing. It was great and by midday, Peter had almost stopped grunting at me and was calling me by my name. Good result I thought. We cleaned and gutted the fish, and went home for a barbeque in the back garden of Peter's house. The next thing I knew I awoke Sunday morning still in my chair! I'd fallen asleep in the garden; Shelly and Peter were asleep in a hammock suspended between two trees. I stood up and good morning hangover! I sat down again fast. It must have been a good night I though and searched the table for something non-alcoholic in an attempt to quench my thirst!

Shelly awoke some half hour later, sat up, moaned and put her head in her hands. "I thought you Aussies were professional boozers?" I said. "Yeah, but not twelve hours at a time," she replied. It was only 8 in the morning and it was already boiling hot. We stayed in the garden all that day, chilling and drinking mostly water, complaining of self-inflicted alcohol induced headaches!

I arrived back at the site at gone 11.30, and said goodbye to Shelly. She said she would get a message to me a couple of days before she next came to Holland. We had a little kiss and cuddle and back I walked slowly towards my cabin. Inside all the lights were on, all the doors open, but nobody was home. Not even Scott! Maybe, I though, they had gone to a local bar and Scott had showed the new lads the way or something. I woke well before 6am and plodded off to the burger van. There was still no sign of anyone. Puzzled, I sat, drank a few cups of coffee, had a bite to eat, grabbed my tools and wandered off to find the Krauts. "Where's Scott?" said Andreas. I just shrugged my shoulders, "Don't know," I said, which I didn't. Breakfast came and went, so did dinner break. Then just before 4pm, I saw three police vans, and two police cars pull up outside Bastiaan's office. Bastiaan jumped out of the first police car with Scott, and the chippies followed from the three police vans. Along with half the Noordwijkerhaut's police force!

I waited, with baited breath for over an hour before Scott came out of the office. He walked straight towards me, he didn't look very happy at all! "Bloody morons," he said. "Where have you been?" I said, which was a bit stupid, as they had obviously just come from the local police station!

Scott began the story. "After you left on Friday night, the new lot," he motioned towards Bastiaan's office, "Asked me where a good place was to go for a night out. I said Noordwijkerhaut had a few good bars and restaurants. I drew them a map and off they went. I sat and watched a bit of TV, went to call Jackie, and then thought I'd have an early night, so I went to bed," he said. "They rolled in blind drunk at gone 4 in the morning, woke me up playing cards or something, and slept all day Saturday. On Saturday evening, they found the colour photo copier machine, next to the medical unit, and had photocopied some high denomination Dutch paper currency and later that evening had returned to the town with all this fake money. They found a brothel and had managed, in the darkness, to pass over 1500 guilders no one had noticed the fake money but the Dutch knew their clients were English and they knew the only English in the area were working not ten kilometres up the road on this building site. The next thing

I knew, I was dragged out of bed at gone three in the morning by two huge coppers, and off we went down to the local nick, with the rest of the bloody idiots." He again motioned towards Bastiaan's office. "They then made us all line up for an identification parade in the police station. Two minutes later, in walked five girls and two taxi drivers to identify the perpetrators. "Bloody hell," I said. "The girls and the taxi drivers picked every one of them out, but excluded me," said Scott, "But the police said to me, they knew I wasn't involved but I still had to stay and make a statement and have my fingerprints taken, just to make sure. They then put me in a cell, and asked me if I had a contact number for someone in authority, as I had a card from Bastiaan's hotel in my pocket, I gave them the number. They called him at four in the morning, and he arrived at just gone 4.30, not looking at all happy. All this time," said Scott, "I still had no idea as to what had happened or why we had all been arrested! Bastiaan had me released from my cell, and made me wait in the foyer. The rest of the lads have been charged with passing counterfeit currency! The police are just getting all their passport details now, from Bastiaan." "Bloody hell!" I said again. "I'm knackered," said Scott, "I'm off to bed, wake me at about eight o'clock will you," and with that he wandered off towards our cabin.

We never saw the chippies from Newbury again. They had left all of their power tools, their clothes and even three cars behind. Bastiaan never said a word to either of us again, so we never knew what the outcome of the event was, but some three or four weeks later the three cars disappeared one night!

It was now halfway through September and it began raining. It got heavier and heavier, we could not work and after it had been raining for over 5 days, the burger vans started closing down, one after the other, until eventually they were all shut. We had to go and get some food, and jumped in the golf. The rain had caused over 3-4 centimetres of water all over the site. Scott couldn't get the car out, we were stuck. We found a forklift and towed the car out of the gooey mud and shot off to Bastiaan and Stella's for food.

Stella insisted we took off our wet clothes and she dried them for us in her tumble drier. She gave us our clothes back after about 15 minutes and asked us why everything was a funny sort of mud green colour. Scott said we hadn't quite got the hang of washing machines yet and now most of our clothes were now much the same colour. "Silly boys," she said and added, "I don't know why you two don't move into the hotel, and I'll do your washing for you." Now why we hadn't thought about this before I'll never know, but we drove back to the site, picked all our shit up and were back at the hotel in less than an hour. We struck a deal with Stella for £50 each a week, including breakfast, and dumped our stuff in our new shiny rooms. It rained every day for nearly two weeks, but we didn't care now. We had TV, video, pool table, darts, a sauna and a swimming pool in the cellar, the bar was self service and Stella was always fussing over us all day long. Things could not have been better, phone calls home became more regular, and we could also get incoming calls on the payphone at the hotel. Jackie was now nearly five months pregnant and now because she could, was phoning Scott every 5 minutes and was driving him up the wall.

The rain stopped as quickly as it had begun, we went back to work. It was over two weeks since we had worked. The Krauts were still on site in their cabins, still looking pristine in their white working gear. I wondered why their clothes weren't a funny colour green, like ours, either they didn't wash their working gear, or they knew how to operate the washing machines!

The site was a mud bath and all the bricks and blocks were soaking, this made them extremely heavy and also because they were wet. They slowly began to wear the skin away on my hands, eventually you wear through the skin. Your fingers begin to crack and bleed from the blocks and cement; gloves only tend to slow the process down a bit, and also make your hands stink. It's painful, but unfortunately happens every year as the weather deteriorates.

No more blue skies and sunshine, October was overcast with high winds and occasional rain. Scott and I were picking up the odd piece of German from the lads at work, and at the time didn't realise how important this was to become in the not too distant future.

My birthday rolled around on the 13th and Scott's, funnily enough, was on the 15th, so we spent the whole weekend celebrating being twenty three years old, in a drunken stupor and trying to decide what we were going to do next year in 1984. Scott and Jackie were planning to get married in the following March after the baby was born, and Jackie had given up her full tie job as an infant teacher, and was working at the White Horse part time.

We only had another eight weeks to go before our contract ran out with Bastiaan. We talked to Bas and asked if it was possible to extend our contract to the end of the next January, he was more than happy to oblige. We started working Saturdays to boost our income and had promised ourselves no more wild weekends, in order to return home with as much money as possible. The days remained fairly mild and rain free until the 17th of November. We got up to find overnight it had snowed. There was ice everywhere and it was freezing. In England you can't lay bricks below three degrees Celsius and the temperature must be rising. In Holland, they make a special mortar; it's hot and contains a frost protector and an accelerator to make it go off quicker. So the good thing was we lost no time at work, the bad thing was we froze to death everyday at work. It was horrible; at least at night we could sit in the sauna and cook ourselves warm again.

Shelly called to say she was going back to Perth with Peter because her father was ill and needed to be cared for. She said she would call and hoped to meet up with me in a couple of weeks. I told Scott the news, he just laughed, "You're jinxed," he said, "Every bird you meet ends up doing a runner on you. You'll be single all your life," he added. December was trauma and drama free both at work and at home. Christmas came and we had a few days off and spent it together with Bastiaan and Stella. It was a great Christmas. Before we knew it, we were packing the golf and getting ready to go home. Bastiaan thanked us and gave us a 1000 guilders bonus each. He said he had work for Scott and me anytime we wanted it, and told us to call him after Easter. Stella hugged us both, nearly breaking every rib in our bodies and made us promise to phone her once in a while. We agreed to do so, and off we went towards the Hook of Holland to get a ferry home.

VII HOME AGAIN

Five and a half hours later, Scott dropped me at my parents' house, said we'd meet up Friday night, and shot off in the direction of the White Horse. I dumped my stuff in the porch and walked in, "Hello dear," said mum, "Have you had a nice day darling?" "Err, yeah," I mumbled. Over seven months had elapsed since I was last at home, I don't think she'd even noticed I'd been gone!

Dad hadn't moved I don't think. He was still stuck in front of the TV watching the grand prix or something about motor racing anyway. I found a pile of letters for me on the mantle piece, chucked them all apart from the one from my bank and one with an Australian stamp on it. I had more in the bank than I had even had in my life. Dad told me to get out of the way, he couldn't see the tele. No hello, no nothing, great I though. I ripped open the letter, it was from Shelly, and it was over 3 weeks old. I read the contents quickly and found a phone number at the bottom. "Dad, can I use the phone please?" I said. No answer, I took that as a yes and dialled the number. Peter answered and without giving me a chance to say anything, said "What bloody time do you think this is to phone someone?" and slammed the phone down, ooops. I checked the time zones in an atlas and found it was nearly 2.00 in the morning in Perth, double ooops.

The following morning I called again and Shelly answered, "Hi," I said. "Oh my god, where are you? How are you?" said Shelly. "Fine," I said, "I got back home yesterday afternoon, and I don't even think my parents had noticed I had been gone!" she said she was still looking after her father, who had had a stroke and was semi-paralysed down one side of his body. He was only 44 years old and wasn't enjoying his condition at all. "What are you going to do now?" she said. "Don't know, maybe take a holiday or something," I said, "Come and visit me if you want to," she said. "Ok, I'll call you when I get a flight and my visa sorted out," I said. I went to the travel agent that afternoon, booked my flight with a two hour stop over in Singapore, and parted with nearly £500 for my trouble.

A week later Scott took me to the airport, his parting words were, "Don't forget my wedding, you're the best man, so get there or you're in big trouble!" "Don't panic, I'll see you the first week in March," I replied.

I don't know about you, but with me, every time I get a long haul flight, I always manage to end up with a big fat, often smelly bloke next to me, with the manners of a pig who will burp and fart, stick his elbows in my ribs and then insist on telling me his life story, including all the operations he's had, why he's been married 6 times and how people always hate fat people, and then they fall asleep and dribble all over you. Today was no exception to the rule. I had a window seat, and

I saw the bloke I knew was going to plonk himself down beside me before he had even found his seat number. Sure enough he shoe horned himself into the seat next to me, "Can you life your arm rest, I need to sit down," he said. I read the safety card and started to read a magazine I'd found in the seat in front of me but it was too late. "Hi," he said, "My name's Eric, I'm Australian, I sell vending machines, I've just been to a convention in London and just sold over two hundred machines this week." God, I thought, you must have also eaten the contents of each one as well. As we taxied down the runway, he babbled on relentlessly about profit margins, projected sales and how much money he was going to earn in commission when he got back home. By now I'd almost lost the will to live and just as I was about to be extremely rude to my new mate Eric, along came an airhostess and gave me some headphones. Peace at last. I turned up the volume to full and that was the end of Eric, well almost!

Eventually we landed in Singapore and trotted off to the next departure lounge to wait for our next flight. I carefully watched to see where Eric was sitting and sat as far away from him as possible. The flight to Perth was only two thirds full and I had a row of seats to myself. I'd bought a book at Singapore and began to read it. I didn't get far and dropped off to sleep. The next thing I knew we were coming in to land. I looked out the window and all I could see were beaches stretching in both directions, up and down the coast. It looked fantastic. I waited for nearly an hour for my bag to come through and at last made my way to the exit. Customs, as usual, were true to form, and I had to unpack and then repack my case, and answer a load of stupid questions. After they let me go, I promised myself I would get my hair cut because since I had grown my hair long, I had instantly become Mr. Big, the international celebrity smuggler and been stopped at every customs hall I'd ever walked through.

Shelly, and to my surprise, Peter met me at the airport and drove me back to their father's house in a place called Fremantle. The bungalow was lovely, with 5 beds and 4 bathrooms, a huge swimming pool and barbeque area, but the best ting was, it had direct access to the beach. It was boiling hot, over 35 degrees Celsius. Shelly and I wandered up the beach for an hour or so, and then returned to the house for eats.

What a place to live, it was fantastic. Perth itself was very cosmopolitan, with high rise accommodation, huge shopping complexes, restaurants, pubs, clubs, the nightlife was great. I could see myself living here no problem, and little did I know at the time, that some twenty three years later, I would be living there, just up the road as well.

The pub scene was much the same as it was at home, apart from the fact that the Aussie guys had little or not respect for the women, and they seemed to sit one side of the pub while the women sat at the other which I found quite strange and in some pubs the men and women had separate bars! Weird. Both Peter and Shelly were intent on showing me the cultural side of Perth, and we spent most of the first week trudging around museums, churches and other places of historical interest, until we had exhausted everything that they thought was worth seeing. I was still sleeping erratically and I was finding it quite hard to stay awake during the day, but I was wide awake all night. So when Shelly suggested we spend some time on the beach, I was right up for it. After the first week, my body clock adapted to the local time and things got better for me. Shelly's dad came back from hospital and now we spent all our time at home, round the pool or on the beach, swimming, surfing and occasionally a bit of fishing. I was really loving it, big time. I began to think of home and Scott's wedding. I had a best mans speech to write and I wanted to get that under my belt before I got home, so I spent two days trying to compact the 8 years I'd known Scott into a ten minute speech, without inflicting too much damage on the future of his marriage!

The following day, Shelly's dad had a heart attack and was rushed into hospital. I didn't see Shelly or Peter for over a week as they had moved into family accommodation at the hospital to be near their father. I was getting bored on the beach on my own, so I tool a bus and did a bit of exploring, mostly pubs unfortunately, but I did manage to meet a few brickies and had a good chat with them about the building game, which was quite nice.

Shelly and Peter arrived back home looking shattered. Their father had had a bypass operation and it had been touch and go for a while. Shelly then told me she had spoken to her company and they were going to give her a job as ground crew at the airport so she could remain in Australia and tend to her father. I selfishly thought to myself, well that's the end of that then. Just my bloody luck.

I only had another 4 days of my holiday left, I'd been in Australia nearly a month and before I knew it, Shelly and I were on our way back to the airport. We promised to stay in touch (yeah right) and I was on my way home again.

I arrived back home on the Monday and was very surprised when my mother actually managed to speak more than one sentence to me, "Hello dear," she said, "did you have a nice time?" and then she said, "Gosh you're very brown." It was almost a conversation! Dad was still comatose in front of the TV, nothing changes I thought and went to bed, I was knackered.

The 1983-84 winter was a cold one, it was still below freezing in March. I checked my car the following morning and found two hoses had split with the ice, I hoped there was no more damage! I called Scott to see what he was doing. I knew he wouldn't be working as it was so cold. Malcolm answered the phone, "He's got his hands full David, with David," he said. "What?" I said, "His new son," he replied. I had completely forgotten about the baby being due. Scott came to the phone and babbled on for about 5 minutes about his new son, I couldn't get a word in edgeways! But I was quite touched he'd named his son after me. Scott had ordered my penguin suit for the wedding and reminded me the stag night was at the White Horse on Friday.

As I still had another six weeks to go before I got my driving license back, I had decided on Friday to walk down to the White Horse, as it would only take me 40 minutes and I couldn't be bothered to take a bus or a taxi. I arrived at 11.00 to help with preparations but it was already in hand. Scott proudly showed me David and their new accommodation that Malcolm had built in the pub, new bathroom, kitchen and bedrooms, very nice it was too. Jackie was pleased to see me and gave me a big hug. She wasn't very mobile as the birth had been caesarean, as baby David was over 8lbs and Jackie is only tiny.

The guests started arriving soon afterwards, and Malcolm and Mary had excelled themselves. The food was great and so was the band. The pub stayed open until the last people left at 6.30, we hit the sack, and the wedding was at 2.30pm. The wedding was held at a lovely church called St Peters, which was a very old, but also a very pretty church. The vicar looked, I thought, almost as old as the church itself and Scott and I were beginning to have a fit of the giggles as he began making his preparations. We had had a quick rehearsal on the Thursday night to go through the procedure and spent most of the time trying not to laugh as the vicar had a terrible lisp. Very cruel I hear you say, but also extremely funny.

The wedding march began, the congregation stood and in walked Jackie looking absolutely fantastic, she walked up to join Scott and I. The vicar began, "Dearly beloved," I had to bow my head because Scott was starting to giggle again. We got through the ceremony without a hitch and spent what seemed like hours having pictures taken outside in the church grounds.

Malcolm, Mary and Jackie's parents had managed to find a hotel with a big enough function suite to house the two hundred and fifty guests and no money had been spared. The food was superb; there was even a toast master who was announcing the best mans speech. Oh bugger, I stood up and looked around, it was quite daunting with so any people there and bloody hell I thought, the vicar's straight in front of me, wearing a silly buck toothed grin and staring straight at me. I had better curb some of the language in the speech I thought! My heart was pounding as I began, but once I got going I was fine. At last I finished, I turned to sit down and saw Malcolm and Scott grinning like little boys, Jackie's mum and dad just sat there with a stunned look on their faces but the rest of the guests were clapping. Job done I thought to myself and waited for my heart to stop trying to jump out of my chest. Now I could have drink at last and so I did, and I did and I did.

The band began to play, and I began to wish that they hadn't, 'tie a yellow ribbon around the old oak tree' began. Oh god, it was going to be like the derby and Joan club, I thought. Scott and I stood at the bar, "Well," I said, "That's the end of the dynamic duo's drinking nights out, you're married now, and that's the end of it." "Nope," said Scott, "We can still have a boys' night out on Fridays at the White Horse, no problem." "I'll wait and see," I said.

Suddenly the band leader announced that the happy couple were leaving, and we all tramped outside to send them off. Malcolm and Mary had a villa in Spain, and Scott and Jackie were off to spend their honeymoon there, without baby David who was staying at home with Mary. I spent the rest of the evening pestering the head bridesmaid but got absolutely nowhere with her. Stuck up bloody cow.

Monday morning I thought I'd better go and find myself a job and I managed to persuade my mum to run me around, from site to site. My mum is only 4'11 tall and in all the time she had been driving, some twenty five years, had not actually got the hang of the clutch or changing gears. As we kangarooed off down the road, I slumped down in the front seat just in case someone I knew recognised me. By the second site I had got a start for the next day, it was also on a bus route, so I would have no problem getting there or back.

Work was predictably boring routine, blocks and bricks all day long but at least I was now earning £62 a day, not bad I thought. Scott returned and the 'A' team was back in business.

Out of the blue, some three or four weeks later, Bastiaan phoned and said he had a new job for us and if we were interested. It was price work, similar blocks and bricks as his last job but this time it was in Germany. We spent three days talking between ourselves before mentioning it to Jackie, who went ballistic. Scott tried to reason with her, but she was not in the reasoning mood. By Friday, she had calmed down and Scott began his best attempt to persuade her that it was a good idea because they needed to buy a house of their own and this was a quick way of raising the deposit. Jackie relented and eventually agreed.

VIII GERMANY

I got my driving license back and repaired the split hoses on my car and had it serviced. We had discussed taking the VW as it was left hand drive but it wasn't really big enough for all the tools and stuff we wanted to take, so we took my car. Mum and dad were on holiday in Greece and I thought I had better phone them and tell them my plans. I phoned the hotel, a Greek man answered. I said "I would like to speak to my parents in room 208." "Yes sir, we have a swimming pool," he replied. "No, room 208," I repeated. "Yes, from eight o'clock until 12.30," he replied. I gave up and left a note on the kitchen table. *Gone to Germany, phone later, love your son!* I wrote.

We got the ferry to Hamburg; it's a twenty four hour overnight trip and a bit like Butlins on water. I'm sure the band that was playing on stage was the same as the one at Scott's wedding, but I said nothing. We arrived in Hamburg and spent over an hour trying to find our way out. After asking for directions in a petrol station, we at last found the road to Berlin, our destination!

We were chatting away when a green and white BMW with blue flashing lights, flew past us and pulled in front. In the back window was a neon sign, it read *HALT*, and began flashing. "Ooops," I said. We slowed down and moved over. The policeman tapped on Scott's window and said "Papier bitte." He then noticed it was an English car and came round to my side. "Engleesh," he said, "Yes," I replied. "Papers pleeeease," he said. I gave him the lot and he spent a good five minutes looking at the documents and eventually began to speak in fairly good English. "German motorway 130kmh," he said, and then pointed at me and said, "You 180kmh follow me please." "Oh shit," said Scott, "Now what?" We followed the police car to the next petrol station. He then motioned for us to follow him and we obliged. He took us to a hole in the wall and said you pay 60DM. I began to argue and Scott butted in and said, "I think we had better pay it." I put my card in and drew out 100DM, and gave him 60. "Receipt," I said, and he just walked off. "That's gone straight in his pocket," I said indignantly. "Don't wind them up," said Scott, "at least that's the end of it." Two hours later we were in Berlin, we found a pay phone and called Bastiaan. No one answered; it just kept ringing and ringing. On the fourth attempt and an hour later, Bastiaan answered at last. "Where are you?" he said. "Berlin," I replied. "Where in Berlin I mean," he said. "Haven't got a clue," I said, "but we've just driven past a big bronze bear with Berlin written underneath it." "Stay there," he said, "I know where you are."

Bastiaan pulled up an hour later, not in the battered old land rover but in a shiny new range rover. "New car," said Scott as he jumped out. "Yes, nice isn't it?" We shook hands, chatted for a few minutes and then we were off. Bas, as usual, was driving like a lunatic at top speed weaving in and out of traffic and lanes, no indicators or anything. Scott was remarking about the scenery and other things, I had no time to look as I was trying to keep up with the nutter in front.

Over an hour later we came to a very sudden halt. We were in the north east of Berlin in a place called Spandau. "I've arranged for you two to stay here," he said as he opened a gate. We walked in past the main house and into the back garden, at the bottom of the garden stood a Scandinavian style wooden house about 10 x 5 metres. He tried the door, it was locked, "The other lads have the key," he said. "Great," I said, and thoughts of the last time we had shared with other people sprang to mind.

"I'll take you to the site," he said "to meet the other lads and get a key; we'll go in my car." Biggest mistake of our lives, it was like driving with a kamikaze pilot. I must have worn a hole in the floor mats, phantom breaking for him, he swore continually all the way there waving his arms and making gestures out of the open window, shouting at anyone that got in the way. We arrived ten minutes later and luckily in one piece. Bastiaan was out of the car and striding off across the site. We got out and began to follow. "He's a bloody nutcase," said Scott, "No wonder his land rover was so dented." We caught up with Bastiaan, he was talking to some lads on the over site. He introduced us and left us to it. Mark and Mickey were from Liverpool and had been there for over ten months. Mark gave us a price list for the various sizes of bricks and blocks, we studied it and reckoned we could make a killing here. He said they finished work in less than an hour and would give us a lift back to our digs. We sat in the gazebo next to an imbis (burger van), and waited and watched the going ons around us. "You two ready?" said Mark half an hour later, and we followed them to the car park. Mark walked up to a brand new Jaguar XJ6 and opened the door. I looked at Scott, "They must be doing ok," said Scott. "Yeah," I said.

We jumped in and ten minutes later we were back at our digs. Mickey showed us around, there were four bedrooms, with two singles in each one, a bathroom, a kitchen and a lounge, all with wooden floors and ceilings. "Its £160 a month per person," he said, "and you can have this room, the other 3 are occupied. There are eight of us altogether, you'll meet the rest of the lads later," he added. We dragged our cases into our room and sat in the lounge talking to Mark and Mickey about the site, the work and the money they were making. Ten minutes later the rest of the lads rolled in, they were all plasterers from Scotland. We said hello and they all totally ignored us. Good start, I thought and raised an eyebrow at Scott.

Mickey said they were going to the Brauhaus in Spandau and if we wanted to come, "Yes," we said, as we also needed to get something to eat. We arrived at the pub fifteen minutes later. It was heaving with Germans but there were more English there than I could count, maybe a hundred and fifty or so, obviously all from the building trade as most of them were still in their working gear. There was a band playing in the corner, and you could not hear yourself think! We got some food and went out into the beer garden which was also heaving, but at least was a bit quieter.

We saw Mark and Mickey circulating around the pub talking to various English guys and all of a sudden they would disappear. "Drug dealers," said Scott, as we watched them walk out the gate, "Hope not," I said, "I don't want to get involved with any of that crap." We watched them repeating the process time and time again, "I don't need and more trips down a foreign police station," said Scott, I agreed.

Just after twelve O'clock, Mark found us and asked if we wanted a lift home, we jumped in and Mark and Mickey were laughing hysterically as we pulled away. "What's so funny?" said Scott. "We've just sold the car again," said Mark, and carried on laughing. "What do you mean?" said Scott. Mickey explained, "This is my dad's car but he's working in the Far East, he let me borrow it to drive to Germany. We go out every Friday night to a different pub, find a drunken Englishman, ask them if they want to buy a nicked car and offer it to them for 3 000DM. someone, eventually after test driving it agrees and we take the money and give them a key, but not the right key. While their bragging about their new car in the pub, we drive off with the car and the money. We've sold it now eighteen times," he added. "So what happens when the person that's bought the car find out who you are and where you live?" asked Scott. "It's not happened yet," said Mickey and began laughing again. The next day Scott and I got to work at 6.40, the rest of the lads were still in bed. We met Bas and got all our E111's sorted out and also got another photo-pass for the site. He then explained what happened next. The banks man who was a German-speaking, Englishman, had a radio. He could talk to the crane driver who would pick up your materials and drop them where you were working. The foreman had set all the walls out; all we had to do was follow the first course of bricks or blocks above. We were responsible for our own scaffolding and also getting our own mortar. "Ok," we said and off we went. We loaded out for two hours, then got some mortar dropped off and went ballistic for the rest of the day. Every piece of internal work that was going to be plastered we marked with our initials D.S. in red spray paint to I.D. it as ours and the face brick work was simple because each gang had its own flank N.E.S.W. So there could be no arguments later about who had built what.

On the trip over, we had talked about the time we would spend away from home this time and had made the decision that as soon as we had made £6000 each we would go back home and start looking for houses. We had also said that we were definitely going to work weekends to boost our income and so reduce the time we had to spend in Germany, and we were going to try and keep away from too many pubs. So for the first six weeks we stayed in, saved our money and we even managed to do some basic, rudimentary cooking for a while. All the while, the rest of the lads were on the town every night causing mayhem everywhere they went, coming home with fantastic stories about wine, women and song mostly. Mark and Mickey had sold the car another two or three times. The Scottish plasterers were all doing much the same as Scott and I, trying to get some money under their belts to take back home with them. We bought a little barbeque and sat out in the back garden most evenings, eating and chatting with the plasterers and having a few beers. In two months, we had managed to save just over £4000 each. Scott and I were well chuffed with the fact that we had saved so much in so short a time. August arrived and the temperature soared into the low 40s. We started working slightly shorter days as the afternoons were getting too hot to work comfortably in. It was also too hot to sleep in our accommodation, and we were sleeping on sun beds in the garden most nights trying to keep cool. The £6000 figure arrived 4 weeks later, we had done it without getting dragged into the situation that most of the Brits seemed to get into, i.e. spending everything they earned and going home with nothing. We had also heard horror stories of people getting ripped off for fantastic amounts of money by the Dutch and Germans, and luckily for us, Bastiaan had proved again he was a genuine employer and paid us every week with no problems at all.

It had been worth living like hermits for thirteen weeks; we had kept our heads down, made our money and kept out of trouble. "Result," said Scott, as we yet again packed the car and made our way back to Hamburg and the ferry. We had not seen anything of Germany in the short time we had spent there, which was a bit of a shame, but we had made the same amount of money we would have made after tax in nine months at home in England.

IX BACK HOME AGAIN

We got off the ferry the following morning and got stopped predictably as usual by customs who made us empty the car our completely and unpack our cases. We got a lecture about carrying sharps but at last they let us go. But then as we left the port, we were stopped by the police yet again. The officer said I had no car tax on my car, I replied "It ran our while we were in Germany." He gave me a producer and let us on our way. Welcome home, I thought as we headed for home. We arrived at the White Horse, left the car and went in. The first thing I noticed was Jackie's bump. I looked at Scott, he just grinned at me. "Bloody hell," I said, "You're a glutton for punishment." We emptied out the car and I drove off home.

I now had over 15K in the bank; it was time to go looking for a house. I took my mother along with me and we drove around looking for new developments in the area. I found a nice two bed house in the small village of Bagshot and parted with 6K as a deposit. It was off plan and would not be finished until April the next year but at least it gave me the opportunity to choose carpet colours, bathroom suits, tiles and wall colourings. Mum, being ever the practical one, suggested because I was a typical bloke, it would be advisable to get everything in dark colours, for example grey, so it wouldn't show the dirt, as she knew I wouldn't be doing a lot of cleaning. So I ordered grey of everything, bath carpets and wall colourings. On the way out of the site, I stopped and got Scott and I a start for the following day. I would now be building a part of my own house.

It was October now, and the weather was starting to deteriorate on a weekly basis. We were working six days a week and as Scott and Jackie had bought a flat on the same development, we though in our own little way, we could help speed up the process of our houses being completed. Scott and Jackie's place was finished in the late part of 1985, which was good timing because the baby, Millie, was born two days after they moved in. my place had not even been started, there was no way it was going to be ready by April, no way at all. The larger houses got priority over the smaller ones because they were more in demand. As my terrace of houses had only been part sold, they had put them on the back burner for a while. At last and with no apology for the delay, I got to move into my house. It was September and five months after the projected completion date. In fact, it was almost a year after I had first put my deposit down!

I had had no idea how expensive it was to furnish a house. I could not believe it, money just disappeared. It cost me a fortune but what annoyed me the most was you ordered something but then you had to wait 3 months for them to deliver it and two months later all I had was a garden shed, a lawnmower, a T.V and video and an airbed I'd bought to sleep on until my bed arrived. Telecom eventually connected my phone and then charged me £399 for the privilege. Cheeky buggers. I started phoning the furniture shops the next Saturday to chase up my now overdue furniture. I started with the bed shop, because by now my back was killing me sleeping on my airbed, which was going down every night. "Oh, we tried to deliver your bed last Monday, Sir, but there was no one in," said the man. "No, I was at work," I replied, "So when can you deliver it," I added. "Wednesday," he said, "What time?" I asked. "Between 8 and 5, Sir," he replied. "Can you give me a more specific time?" I said, "I'm self employed and don't really want to take the whole day off." "Sorry Sir," he said, "It will be between 8 and 5, that's the best I can do." Great, I thought, I took Wednesday off and sat in front of the T.V on my old deck chair my dad had given me, and waited and waited. At 4.00 I called and exploded down the phone at the poor girl who answered. She promised it would be there before the end of the day. At 6 O'clock I called again and left a rather rude message on their answer-phone and walked around to Scott's. I was fuming when I got there and as I walked in the kids were screaming blue murder. Scott and I left Jackie to it and walked down to the Kings Arms pub in the village. "I'll tell Jackie," said Scott, "She can deal with it for you." "Thanks," I said. Two weeks later I had all of my furniture delivered and Jackie, bless her, dealt with it all on my behalf.

Christmas came and went, January was a cold one, and we found ourselves only working for a few hours a day, which meant very, very poor wages. Over the next few weeks we spent more time in the pub than we did at work and at one stage had ten consecutive days without any work at all. We had been better off financially when we had been renovating pubs some four years ago and with that in mind, the following day spent all day on the phone phoning all the local breweries trying to find out who was doing their work and if it was possible to have a number to call so we could get a job. I called Courage Brewery and ended up speaking to the contracts manager, who after a short conversation asked me if we were interested in pricing some work for them. I agreed and 3 days later received two set of drawings in the post. We found a local quantity surveyor who priced them up for us and we returned the whole package to Courage's. Just as we were about to give up on a reply, I received a phone call asking us to attend a meeting in Reading the following week!

We turned up all suited and booted. An hour later we walked out with two extensions and a demolition job to start in ten days time. The White Horse was our next port of call to celebrate our good fortune. We sat in Malcolm's office in the pub and panicked. We only had £800 between us and the old VW golf in the garage.

We part exchanged the golf against a second hand transit tipper and financed it over 3 years, bought an old cement mixer from exchange and mart, opened an account with a local builders merchant, and bought a ready made LTD company. We also opened a business account. The first job was the demolition of an outside toilet block. The pub was Victorian, so we saved the bricks and made £1100 selling them to a local re-claim yard. We put in our invoice and received our first cheque at the end of the month, and with the money we paid the finance off the transit and bought some much needed new power tools.

The second job was an extension, Scott and I did the ground work and the brick and block work. The rest we subcontracted out, chippies, plumbers, sparky's and plasterers. The third job was underway before the second was even finished. Another job had been offered to us and we priced and got it. Things were happening fast now and because we wanted to be successful, Scott and I were working very long hours, including most weekends. Jackie was doing our books and most of the material ordering, but six weeks later, we had another two jobs to start, and had to start employing some labour full time.

It had all taken off at an alarming rate; we were drawing a wage of £350 a week each now, and didn't have time to spend any of it. Jackie was complaining to Scott that she hardly ever saw him anymore. I hadn't had time to find myself a new girlfriend either. How sad I hear you say?!

Two more jobs arrived the following week and things began to get crazy. We had to employ yet more labour to reduce the hours we were working. We found a small brickwork gang, two brickies and a hoddy, which was great. Scott and I started the ground work and completed up to D.P.C and the new gang built from damp to plate on a price. This put us back on an even keel, we could relax a bit and now at last, and now some five months later, have the odd weekend off.

The transit packed up on the way to work, and after open engine surgery, it was time to put it out of its misery because it was going to be too expensive to put right. We bought a brand new shiny one, a tipper on lease purchase, £140 a month with £500 down. Even the wipers worked on this one, it was great. We spent the next 3 weeks arguing over who was going to drive to work each day.

Including the two of us, we now we're a team of 7 people, including all the sub-contract labour that came and went as they were required. The wage bills each week were growing and growing. I could not believe that less than 7 months ago we had been sat in a pub just talking about getting back into pub renovation and now it was us that was doing it for ourselves and also employing people to work for us. We didn't turn a job down and because of that we were now working further a field, and found ourselves as far away as Kent in one direction, and Essex in another. As October rolled around we decided to have a week off and let the lads get on with it, after all we had hardly had a day off for ten months. We chose the week of our birthdays. I cut the grass in my back garden for the first time in months and tidied up the garden as it was starting to look like a builder's yard.

We went out for a meal to celebrate our birthdays and also our good fortune. Jackie and Scott announced they were expecting again, but I wasn't listening, I was too busy looking at our waitress, Louise, it said on her badge. She was lovely. I paid for the meal and at the same time asked Louise out for a drink. Two days later we went to a wine bar in Weybridge for a drink. Louise was twenty one and at uni doing a business degree and was waitressing to supplement her grant. Just three months later my mouth ran away with me and without consulting my brain asked her if she would like to move in with me. And that was the end of my little world, no more slobbing out on the settee watching football with Chinese, or an Indian take away, no more dirty cups in the sink, no more sleeping on the settee with the TV on all night and waking up lying in my pizza from the night before. She then said, "And as for the colour scheme of this house, that will all have to change." What had I done, before I knew what had hit me, I had spent another small fortune and Louise had turned my house into an advert for Laura bloody Ashley. Pink this, fluffy that, smelly things all around the house. I had even had to change the colour of the carpets to match all the stuff she had insisted that I bought. It didn't stop there; she then went totally Charlie Dimock in the garden as well. At last it stopped, but now it was finished to her satisfaction. I was told to take my work boots off outside before I came into my own house. I could feel a row brewing. Just as I was about to completely freak out, the doorbell rang.

It was Scott and Jackie, with two little demons in tow. Jackie loved the new look in the house and her and Louise started on a grand tour. Scott and I escaped into the garden, "Looks nice," said Scott, and burst out laughing. "I was quite happy with it the way it was," I replied.

We talked about work we had starting the next week as we had just begun our biggest job to date. It was a huge function suite some 20m x 12m and had to be completed in just thirteen weeks from start to finish. We also had our first year accounts to get ready and Jackie was finding it hard to keep up with the books and looking after her two children at the same time, and with another due in less than two months, it was not fair to expect her to either. We hired a book keeper to keep up with the ever increasing number of receipts and delivery slips, which we had to deposit with her on a weekly basis to keep us from losing a majority of them.

Jobs were coming in on a weekly basis now, some big and some fairly small. The small ones often were more profitable as you were in and out in one or two days and may be only doing simple plumbing repairs, or changing locks when the premises changed hands. We bought another vehicle and gave it to our now full time, small works gang, a plumber and his mate.

Baby Clare entered the world at the beginning of March and Scott took a week off to be with Jackie. He also put his house on the market as now a new house was definitely required. It sold after it had been on the market for 3 days. Eight weeks later they had moved another road closer to me and now had 4 bedrooms and a double garage. Louise visited Jackie and Scott's new house and on her return started going on about the benefits of having a bigger house. I told her she was wasting her breath, we were staying put and that was that. We moved into our new house diagonally opposite Scott and Jackie's 4 months later. I converted the garage into an office and we bought a fax machine and put a separate phone line into the garage. The new office soon became Scott's retreat from the joys of fatherhood and we'd spend many evenings sitting there with a few beers pretending to price jobs up and were not to be disturbed at any cost.

Louise was still at university and still had nearly a year to go, she had also stopped waitressing and I was now subsidising her, the amounts she required were going up on a weekly basis. She insisted most of it was for books and transport to and from uni. I gave her the ford in a vain attempt to keep my bank account in credit and it seemed to slow my problem down for a few months. Then her parents, who were working in some capacity for the air force, had to move up to Scotland and all of a sudden I had a new lodger, Laura her sister, along with 3 cats, a Yorkshire terrier called Bob, and a bloody African grey parrot called 'Squawk.' After just only 5 minutes, I knew how this stupid bird had got its name, its just squawked and squawked non stop. The only time it shut up was when it was eating. I decided this bird was either going to end up being the fattest African grey in the world or a very dead parrot.

By the end of the week Laura's boyfriend began paying visits and I began to get more and more agitated by the string of events that had led up to this situation. As I left for work the next morning, nothing could have prepared me for what awaited me when I got home that evening. The driveway was full so I parked on the road and walked in. Louise's parents had decided to pay us a visit for the weekend without any warning whatsoever. They had arrived with the two Labradors, Bes and Ben, two sets of golf clubs and now I had a zoo in my house. I'd also been booted out of my bedroom. Then just as I though it couldn't get any worse, Duncan, Laura's boyfriend turned up on his scooter. I now had dogs chasing cats, dogs chasing dogs, parrots squawking, cats climbing the curtains and Laura and Duncan having a blazing row. I walked into the kitchen to find Louise and promptly tripped over a set of golf clubs and went head long. Twenty seconds later I was banging on Scott's door, as he opened the door I said, "Pub now!" As we walked past my house the noise was deafening. No one had noticed me leaving the house. We arrived at the pub and two minutes later I phoned Louise from a phone box. "I'm so sorry," she said, "It doesn't matter," I replied, and added I was staying at the pub until her parents went to bed or closing time. "Ok," she said and hung up. We left the pub at 11.30 and rolled home. Peace eventually returned to my house on Sunday afternoon. Louise's parents thanked us for a lovely weekend, and as they left said they hoped to see us again very soon. Not if I can fucking help it, I said under my breath.

The Anchor pub was on the venue Monday morning and five minutes after we arrived, Scott went upstairs to see how the chippies had got on with a new floor we were putting in. He trod on a floor joist that wasn't fixed and fell; he hit his chin on the joist, then continued down between the joists and landed on the floor right beside me on a pile of brick rubble. The air went blue for over ten minutes. I helped him into the van and headed for the neared hospital, which was in Portsmouth. He had broken his leg in two places and also fractured his jaw on the floor joist. I phoned Jackie from the hospital and gave her that bad news, he was going to have to stay in over night to check for concussion and spend most of the following day to have his jaw wired or something equally as horrible. I drove down with Jackie again the following morning and we waited with Scott. His leg had now been set and plastered but his face was black and blue. According to the doctor he had also broken his nose. Eventually after 4 hours waiting, he went to face the music and also the pain that was without fail going to go with it.

"I've got to stay in overnight again," he said as he walked toward us, his face looked terrible. "That looks like it hurts," I said, "Can't feel a thing," said Scott flicking his chin with his finger. "You nutter," I said. All in all, Scott was in hospital for 3 days and after that he spent another 7 weeks at home before he was fit enough to come back to work again, but it was mid-October before he felt well enough to drive again. In the two months he'd been convalescing, he had managed to get Jackie pregnant yet again, the loony!

The month or so before Christmas and also the January after tend to be a bit slow in the pub renovation game because the publicans don't want their pubs disrupted during the Christmas and New Year period as it would obviously affect their trade. As Christmas time is often one of the busiest times of the year for them, we found ourselves twiddling our thumbs by the middle of November. Scott and his tribe went on holiday to his father's villa in Spain and I decorated my house. I hate decorating with a passion; I'd rather suffer a hangover every day and night for a week. I'd even go shopping to Sainsbury's with Louise, push the trolley and keep my mouth shut all day, rather than pick up a paintbrush and roller. I always get covered in it, I hate it. Get the picture? The two weeks of painting ended at last, and the suicidal tendencies started to diminish.

Scott and Jackie returned on the Saturday afternoon, they opened their front door and the place was full of water. Scott thought he had turned his central hearing down to frost protect position but in fact he had turned it off. The cold water tank had split, the house was a wreck. Ceilings gone, carpets soaking, the kitchen units had exploded as they were chipboard; everything was ruined. Jackie was in tears. We tried to salvage what we could and they moved into my house that evening. The loss adjusters arrived and some 3 weeks later the crew arrived to start repairing Scott's house. Plasterboard, carpets, everything was skipped, some electrics were stripped out, the furniture was also skipped and then they brought in the de-humidifier machines to dry the house out. Christmas was only a week away now and the de-humidifiers were to remain in his house nearly 4 weeks long before it had eventually dried out sufficiently for the repairs to begin. Christmas arrived and my house was full, 5 adults, one with a bump developing very rapidly, 3 kids, 3 cats, a dog and the bloody parrot, which was by now treading on very very thin ice.

As Louise's cooking skills had yet to be seen in any way shape or form, we had booked a restaurant for Christmas dinner in the village. It was a bit expensive but nonetheless very enjoyable. The rest of the afternoon we spent at home watching the Dam Busters and the Great Escape, which brought back memories of another little camp we had visited in Holland.

The first week of January I received a letter from my mortgage company telling me the interest rates would be going up by 0.5%. This was the first of many letters I would receive over the next few months, bearing news of more impending interest rises.

Work began to come in quite slowly, but by the end of January

1988, we had enough to keep us buys for the next 7-8 months. Scott moved back into his house at the end of February which cheered Jackie up no end as by now she was getting quite big in the belly region and finding it hard to move around with so many people in one house. More letters were arriving from the mortgage company and the tabloids were forecasting doom and gloom for the coming year, babbling on about consumer spending having to be curbed or we were heading for a recession!

Work began coming in again and we found ourselves doing the headless chicken thing again, running between 3-4 jobs a day. The mileage we were doing each week was fantastic and before long we were back working Saturdays and Sundays again trying to get back in front and keep the publicans happy by turning the jobs around as quickly as we possibly could. We were now employing 7 people again and the wage bills were getting bigger and bigger each week, but we couldn't complain. We put our own wages up to £80 a day but only paid ourselves a maximum of £400 a week, regardless of whether we worked the weekend or not. We needed another vehicle as it was becoming far too time consuming picking up and dropping off cement mixers and other plant for the brickies, so we went to the car auctions to buy them a second hand pickup. I went to the toilet and left Scott to bid on anything that was in our price range. When I came back I asked him if anything had taken his fancy. He said "Yes, lot 29." I walked out the auction hall to see what we had bought; Scott had bought an old 1967 split screen bloody VW camper! I had to laugh, it was a heap of crap but he drove it home and put it in his garage. We never did get to buy a pickup that day. Jackie went ballistic when he got it home and said that they had better things to spend their money on than twenty year old rust buckets, but Scott was smitten. He had his VW camper again and no matter what anyone said, he was going to renovate it.

That evening I got home to find Louise and Laura sitting on the settee booing their eyes out. "What ever is wrong?" I said. "Its squawk," replied Laura, "I let him out for his daily fly around and one of the cats has caught him and killed him." "Stop grinning David," said Louise, "It's not funny." I just thought result, one down five to go, and went into my office for a beer and a giggle to myself.

The following Saturday Scott asked me to give him a hand to get his camper to the body shop for a shot blasting and a few new panels. The problem was it wouldn't start and could I tow him to the garage with our van. After I had at last stopped laughing I agreed and we struggled to push the beat up old camper out of the garage and onto the road. We tied a rope between the two and off we went. As we pulled away I saw Scott waving at me from behind. I didn't have a clue as to what he meant, but I soon found out as I got to the next roundabout, I had to give way and stopped. The problem was Scott behind me couldn't stop; the brakes on the camper had seized up solid. He crashed straight into the back of the tipper with a loud band and stopped dead. I couldn't breathe for laughing and eventually Scott began to see the funny side and started to laugh as well. We shortened the rope between the two vehicles and wedged two bales of cavity insulation between the truck and the VW and continued on our way.

The first thing George at the body shop said to Scott was, "Do you really, really want to spend the kind of money on this that it is going to cost to get it back into shape?" "Yep," said Scott and that was that. Nearly £900 changed hands and off we went. The camper arrived back at Scott's three weeks later, with new front doors, new side doors, a complete new front end, new bumpers front and rear. It had also been shot blasted and sprayed in grey primer. Scott went to work on the engine. I couldn't even persuade him to venture down the pub with me for over three weeks, in which time he had spent another small fortune in the process. It now ran perfectly, it also had the ability to stop thanks to new brakes all round.

He then started on the interior and completely stripped everything out, and once finished off it went for a respray. It came back two days later a very nice deep red colour. Next a specialist company that dealt with VWs went to work and re-trimmed the interior to the original specification. It was now finished at last, he had spent over £4000 on it, but it now looked an exact replica of his old one and he was absolutely chuffed to bits with it. To celebrate, we all went down to the New

Forrest in if for the day.

On the way back home, Jackie started complaining of severe stomach pains. We found the nearest hospital and charged in. Louise and I were left with the kids and Scott followed Jackie in to see a doctor. The pains turned out to be premature labour and before we knew what was going on, baby Chloe was delivered six weeks early. Two hours later we all went in to see mother and baby. Chloe was tiny but healthy in an incubator next to Jackie's bed. Jackie and Scott were ecstatic with her. "One boy, three girls," I said, "Think of the cost of all those weddings mate!" "The more the merrier," Scott replied, the bloody loony!

When baby Chloe came home some three weeks later, Louise and I went round to Scott's to wet the baby's head. By now, Chloe had discovered her lungs and was using them to her full advantage. She just screamed and screamed 24/7. She was without a doubt the loudest baby I've ever encountered. A week later, with no sleep, Scott was beginning to look extremely tired and because of that, also a bloody grumpy bastard with it. He would walk out the house most mornings looking like a panda, his eyes had dark black rings around them. It began to affect his work and on one occasion, actually while he was driving the van to work, he fell asleep. The impact was at a slow speed, luckily, and the damage to the van was fairly minor. We had our first row in over eleven years and standing on a roundabout in the middle of High Wycombe, began to punch the living daylights out of each other.

It only lasted a few minutes but by the time we had finished, there were black eyes and split lips, broken teeth and bleeding noses. Eventually we got back into the van and drove for the next ten minutes in total silence. "You bloody hit me," said Scott, suddenly scowling at me. "You started it," I retorted. "Yeah, but you didn't have to hit me," he said. Silence reigned again for another twenty minutes.

I put a cigarette in my mouth and tried to light it but where my lip was split, every time I sucked on the cigarette, it wouldn't light and all I could manage was to make this farting noise with my mouth. Scott began laughing. Ten seconds later I had to stop the van; we were now both totally in pieces laughing hysterically like two little kids on the side of the road.

After a few minutes we managed to eventually stop laughing. "I'm sorry," I said to Scott, "I didn't mean to hit you; it was just that you wound me right up, mate." "Mates don't need to apologise," he replied, and that was the end of our first and also our last fight with each other, but not our last fight!

The office at home now was becoming very popular, for two reasons now. One was Scott was using it as a retreat from the noise that passed for normal family life at his house, and two, Louise was about to do her finals at uni and was constantly studying and revising at home, she always had her head stuck in a book or was watching a video about business related stuff, which looked quite complicated so I left her to it and Scott and I remained in the office 'pricing up work.'

Louise had already been for a few interviews in London and had, depending on her results, been offered a job with a company that had something to do with updating share index prices on the stock exchange.

Scott and I were enjoying the peace and quiet, we now had a TV in the office and a video, so we spent most evenings sitting watching TV, beers in hand, cocooned in our own little environment, oblivious to all the problems and noise at Scott's house, and the zoo next door with Louise and Laura making more noise than a small nuclear explosion every night.

WINDING DOWN!

My first indication that things in the building industry were starting to slow down came along a couple of months later. The interest rates were now climbing very steadily, almost on a monthly basis. My mortgage was now heading into orbit. The wages Scott and I were paying ourselves were becoming an issue. Scott had obviously more money to pay out with four small children in the house and we decided to pay ourselves another £100 a week to try and alleviate the problem.

Both Scott and I began receiving phone calls from friends in the industry asking if we had any work for them and some of our sub-contractors were also complaining that the work was beginning to dry up quite quickly, and to add insult to injury, the main contractors were starting to reduce the day rates and prices in order to remain competitive and in business.

The spiralling down effect was all of a sudden happening very, very quickly indeed. We only had two jobs running, and Scott and I had begun to start worrying about the situation ourselves. It was now out of control. Things were going form bad to worse, and according to the press and politicians, we were now heading for a recession!

We had two jobs come in and with the drawings came a letter asking us to price the work but allow for a margin to negotiate the end price. We were only a small outfit and our profit margins were only quite small but nonetheless we obliged with the request and two weeks later found ourselves at head office with three other contractors. After the meeting Scott and I discussed it in the van, and there was no way we could knock another 8% off our price as we would be working on a 3% profit margin and that was unacceptable. "If we don't do it," said Scott, "We will have no work." "If we do actually do it and we have one or two overheads we haven't accounted for, we will be working for nothing!" I said.

We got back home and sat in the office thrashing out the profit margins to see if we could manage to meet the price guidelines. In the end we decided to submit the reduced price and take a chance that nothing went wrong and hope we still came out on top!

We needn't have bothered, because one of the other contractors had reduced his prices to a point where even Scott and I could not compete, he must have been doing if for nearly nothing. Now we had a major problem on our hands. We both had mortgages which were going up and up and up, the interest rates were bordering on 13% now and my mortgage had nearly doubled in the past 7 months. We also had the tipper on lease purchase, and a few items of plant we had also bought.

I had not realised how quickly everything was happening. The knock on effect was charging through the building industry at an alarming rate. It was now affecting all trades. Bricklayers were going on site asking the sub-contractors what they were paying and then offering to work for £5-10 less a day. This resulted in other people being sacked. It was becoming very cut throat, fights were breaking out on a regular basis and it was going to get worse, much worse.

We needed work, so Scott and I started cruising all the local sites in our van. We spent the first day with no results at all, the second day we travelled further a field and still got nothing, or got 'I'll take your number and if anything comes up, I'll give you a call." Yeah right!

The pubs were now full of builders, plasterers, sparky's and plumbers all having the same type of problem, but sitting in pubs spending more money was not the answer to the problem. We managed to get a start in Portsmouth, which was over 60 miles away at £52 a day and I said to Scott, "We were earning this money when we first finished our apprenticeship!" "Yeah," he said, "But it's better than nothing."

After the first month, neither of us had earned enough money to pay our mortgages, let alone pay for the van, bills or anything else. I was getting very worried indeed.

I sold Louise's car, which really annoyed her but at least we had enough money to pay the food bills and the following months' mortgage. I got peanuts for the car as no one wanted to stretch themselves financially, but at least it stopped me panicking for a while.

The following month the interest rates went up again, and I had to find another £90 to put towards my ever increasing mortgage. Then the quarterly bills came in and I nearly had a baby! How the hell was I going to pay all this, credit cards became my saviour, at least it gave me another month to try and get some money together to pay them off.

The site Scott and I were working on had banned vans, pickups, and tippers like our on site because too much stuff was being stolen from the site by people trying to supplement their income by selling stolen materials. Then we got our company tax bill. This was game over, between us we had nothing and after speaking to the tax office and our accountant, we found we had no option but to pay it! We approached our bank for a business loan, but the repayments were hideous. So we both decided to pay half each on our credit cards, which looking back was even more expensive in the end, but nonetheless, we had at last paid the tax bill.

Louise got her degree and began work in London. The next problem that raised its ugly head was how was she going to get there without a car? I bought her season ticket from Bagshot to London and spent £1500 in the process, but at least she was working now and I was looking forward to her being able to contribute towards the cost of running the house. Although her first priority was to pay off her student loan so most of what she was earning was going straight back to the bank! She was not going to be able to give me any money towards the mortgage, or any bills!

My problems began to get steadily worse, and I found myself drawing money out the bank on a credit card to put towards the costs of the house. All I was doing was compounding the problem weekly. Scott was also having major problems financially and we began to think the worst. If it carried on much longer we would end up having both our houses re-possessed. Something had to be done and done fast.

The following day, Scott and I talked about going back to work for Bastiaan and that night when we returned home I phoned him. There was a' no number' signal. I tried the hotel and was told by the lady who answered the phone that Bastiaan and Stella had sold it to them over six months ago and she also had no knowledge of their new address or telephone number. We sat Louise and Jackie down and went through our plan. Louise was to move in with Jackie and the kids; I would rent my house out and split the proceeds with Scott and Jackie. Then Scott and I were going to go back abroad and try and dig us both out of the hole we had managed to dig ourselves into! The girls were going crazy, but eventually they saw the logic behind it and as neither of them wanted to be homeless, relented and agree it was the best solution.

GERMANY AGAIN

Scott left Jackie with the camper to drive and also a list of instructions which included where and where not she could park it, and how to drive it. Don't spill petrol on the paintwork…the list was endless and also, I thought, a bit of a cheek really, but at least she had transport and could get out and about. We packed the tipper with our tools and enough clothes for a couple of weeks, said our goodbyes and headed for the ferry. We arrived at Harwich and joined the queue waiting to board. We were in the panel van and small truck queue and as we looked around we noticed that a large majority of the vehicles were builders' vans, sign written with various company names and logos. Everyone was literally in the same boat as Scott and I and were trying to do the same as us, trying to save what they had worked so hard for by leaving their families and friends and going abroad, hoping above all that this was going to save their houses.

We boarded at 7 and found our way straight to the bar, which was full of builders from all walks of life, all with the same idea. Most of them had long faces and didn't look too happy at all to be there. Scott and I had decided to head for Berlin again as it was a large city and we also knew a little bit about the area or the suburbs at least, and on docking at Hamburg, found our way without any problem to the motorway. The last time in the car had taken less than two hours, but with the tipper the progress was much, much slower. We arrived in Berlin at gone 11.30pm and started looking for a cheap hotel to stay in. at last after nearly an hour we found a small pension (hotel) at just 30DM a night, about £10 and booked ourselves in. we dumped our stuff in our rooms and as the hotel bar was still open, came downstairs for a few beers.

The bar was full, totally full of English, Polish and only a few Germans. In less than ten minutes we had between us managed to get over fifteen different telephone numbers of people looking for English bricklayers and most of them were paying between 30-35DM an hour. Things were looking up already. We went outside to find a payphone and called Jackie and Louise just to tell them that we had arrived safely and also managed to find a bed for the night. Louise just moaned for ten minutes about the noise Scott's kids were making and couldn't she just move back into our house, and she also said Laura was fuming that she had to move to Duncan's along with her menagerie. I pointed out she had lived with us for ages and hadn't contributed to anything at all and quite honestly I said, "I don't know what she's got to complain about at all." Louise just slammed the phone down and that was that. "Goodnight, sweetheart," I said, as I replaced the receiver in its cradle.

Sleep that night was almost impossible, because it seemed to me that Berlin did not sleep. The noise was horrendous, cars flying up and down the streets, people shouting and screaming non-stop, the bars were also still open and the nightclubs were creating a dull thud that was even rattling the glass in my window. At some time AM I fell asleep only to be woken, what seemed like two minutes later, by Scott thumping on my door? "Come on, get up, its eight O'clock, lets go!" he said.

Breakfast was not included in the price of the pension, so the next port of call was McDonalds for coffee and egg McMuffins. Yuck, but it had to be done. We found a payphone and I rang the first number on our list, a guy called Paul from Leicester answered. "We're looking for a start mate," I said, "Do you need a couple of bricklayers?" "Yes," he replied. "What are you paying?" I asked. "Thirty five DM an hour," he said. "Where's the job? I asked. "Keith Sts," he said, "Right in the centre of Berlin. "We're actually staying in the same street," I said. We arranged to meet him in an hour and trotted back the way we had just come, feeling quite pleased with the result.

We met Paul an hour later; he seemed alright and after introducing ourselves, followed him up the street. The job was no more than fifteen minutes walk from our pension. We wandered around the job, it was a renovation job. The building had been empty since the war and it used to be an old Jewish slaughter house. Paul introduced us to the polier, the German site agent/come foreman, and after a brief conversation in German, he walked up to Scott and I and shook both our hands. "So

113

what are we doing here?" I asked Paul. "Blocking in doorways, and building new walls to support the floors that will be going in and once that's done you will be cladding the whole of the old building with a new skin of brickwork," he said. "So how long do you think the job will take?" asked Scott. "Oh, about 4 months," replied Paul. "Sounds just the ticket," I said.

There were just two other brickies there already and also four shuttering chippies, all English and all working for Paul. It looked like we had landed on our feet on our first try. Paul said we could also work on Saturdays to boost our wages. Scott and I worked it out, and with a full week we would be earning the best part of £800 and even paying for our hotel and living expenses, we would still be able to send back home over twice what we could currently earn in England before tax. It felt as if a huge weight had been miraculously taken off my back, I wasn't going to loose my house after all. What a relief.

We thanked Paul and told him we would see him at 7 O'clock Monday morning and headed for the nearest payphone to give Jackie and Louise the good news. Louise was at work, but Scott had quite a long conversation with Jackie and I could hear him making cooing noises down the phone, so he must have also had a good chat with the kids too.

We walked back to the van, and drove up to our new job. We took all our tools out and put them into a lockup container that one of the

114

bricklayers had a key for, and had a good chat with the other lads. Simon was the foreman as he spoke really good German and Ray was his sidekick. We had a long talk with the pair of them. They had been working for Paul for nearly two years with only a few hiccups with the money. Paul had kept them in work all the time and Simon said he had more work coming up, so it wasn't worth going chasing the big money, or working for some of these big sub-contractors as a lot of the English were getting stitched up for a lot of money, and not just by the English companies, but also by the Dutch and German firms. And at least with Paul, you knew where you stood, plus if there were any problems, you only had one person to deal with, which in Simon's view, made everything a lot simpler for everyone.

We walked back to our hotel and with the help of a phrase book and by drawing a few pictures, eventually managed to book both our rooms for a month. Well, we thought we had anyway. We now had the rest of the Friday and the whole of the weekend in which to explore the historic city of Berlin. We started off smack bang in the middle of Berlin by the church, which the English had bombed in the Second World War The Germans had left it as it was, but made it water light again and covered it in blue and coloured glass, but from the outside, it still looked as If the bombing had almost just occurred. Not being religious, we walked on by and some ten minutes later, saw a neon sign flashing 'Irish Pub.' "What the hell, lets go and have a beer," said

Scott.

We walked into a shopping centre and followed the arrows pointing the direction of the Irish pub, and walked down two flights of steps into probably one of the biggest pubs I've ever been into. It was about 28m x 20m with the bar running the full length of the room on the left side and going into an L shaped alcove at the opposite end of the pub. It was huge, and also absolutely full of people which I found quite strange as it was only 12.30.

We fought our way through the masses and at last made it to the bar. "Two beers please," I said. "Small or large?" the waitress replied. "Better make them large," I said. The beers arrived and we found our way to an empty spot. It was very strange, although we were away from home again in a foreign country, the weight that had been lifted off my shoulders so quickly by coming to Germany, had suddenly made me feel quite different because of many reasons. I wasn't at home to answer the phone from the bank or credit card firms asking me when and how much I was going to pay them and when exactly was I going to get my account back into credit. There were no letters dropping through my letter box threatening me with court action for non-payment of gas or electric bills. In fact, there was nothing at all because I was in Germany and no one could even get hold of me. I felt great, Louise was now at the sharp end, it was her turn to do something for me and she was just going to have to deal with it!

Scott was feeling much the same way and although we were missing home, the girls and in Scott's case, his kids, it was such a nice feeling considering all the stress and worry that had gone on for the last eleven months. To be, at last, in a position to do something about it financially and also to be free of the continual worry of what you would find on the doormat, or on the answer phone when you got home at night! The pressure was gone and we were going to enjoy it. Yippee!

We sat in the Irish pub all afternoon and by about 5 O'clock, the workers started to wander in, most of them still in their work clothes. Now the pub was packed solid and I think 80% were English. The whole place was alive with people drinking and having a good time. It was great fun this pub, and Scott and I were really having a good laugh.

We got talking to a few lads and an hour later we were heading off to some restaurant with them for something to eat. We had discovered we were in a shopping centre called the Europa Centre, it was full of shops and restaurants from all over the world, and also two or three different pubs but they all agreed the best of which was the Irish pub!

Ian and his sidekick Steve were from Guildford, just down the road from Scott and me, and had been in Berlin for just over eighteen months. They knew all the good companies to work for and gave us a list of names and numbers should we choose to use them. The evening was flying by and before we knew it, it had gone midnight. I hadn't called Louise and Scott had not phoned Jackie either, oops! I said to Scott I was going to hit the sack. He agreed with me but Ian and Steve had other ideas.

We were off to a nightclub called Big Eden, and before we knew what was happening, we were inside. There were three floors and half a dozen different bars inside. We hit the nearest bar and ordered our drinks. Next to us asleep, with their arms on the bar, were three blokes and stacked 4 deep in front of them were about fifteen full glasses of beer. "Obviously very drunk indeed," I said to Scott. "Yeah," he said, "Lets make sure we don't get into such a state!"

As Scott finished speaking, two of the waitresses appeared behind the three lads with a pair of scissors each in their hands, and began to systematically cut the lads' clothes off them with their scissors. The whole process took them about 5 minutes; the three lads had not even flinched, as they were that drunk. They now only had on their shoes and underpants and by now a crowd was standing behind watching the fun develop. Next, the two waitresses went back behind the bar and reappeared with three ice buckets full of cold water and ice. They then poured each bucket over each of the three lads. It was hilarious. The first two didn't move but the third was very suddenly wide awake again. He stood up, promptly fell over, picked himself up again and went stumbling off in the direction of the dance floor, completely oblivious of the fact that all he was wearing was his underpants. The remaining

118

two lads were now receiving their second bucket of ice water each, and all attention was now focused in that direction to see what was going to happen next! "I'm going to like this city!" I said to Scott, but he was too busy laughing to hear what I had said. The other two lads were now both awake again and strangely had not noticed that they were almost naked. They people standing watching the whole thing, were now in fits of laughter. I couldn't believe it, now they were awake again, the first thing they both did was pick up a drink and started drinking again!

The nightclub was full of American, French and various other soldiers in uniforms, mostly standing against bars and walls watching the women dancing around the various dance floors, waiting for their chance to pounce on some poor unsuspecting woman. There was also a large amount of Turkish lads roaming around, and I noticed that most of them seemed to be dishing out, what looked to me, like drugs. I mentioned it to Scott and we both thought it a good idea to make our way to the exit and then back to our hotel, after all, it was almost 4 O'clock in the morning!

After more than half a dozen wrong turns, we eventually found our way back to our hotel, only to find the front door firmly locked up tight as a drum, and no night porter or even a doorbell to ring. So, that was that. It wasn't a cold night as it was still the end of August, but even so, we were both tired and also a bit drunk and needed a bit of sleep.

There was nothing more to do other than head back to the Europa Centre and hopefully the Irish pub would still be open so at least we would be able to get a coffee and somewhere to sit down for a while. As we arrived, the bouncers were just chucking the last of the revellers out of the Irish pub, so that, was also that!

We wandered the streets for nearly two hours before the cafes and small shops began to open up for trade again. By this time, we were tired and very, very hungry. We found a little Turkish imbis and waded through at least six cups of coffee each before we started to wake up a bit. I could feel the beginnings of a hangover starting to kick in. I wasn't looking forward to this because I knew it was going to be a nasty one. It was time to eat something full of fat and grease in order to keep the hangover at bay. Both Scott and I forced a couple of German sausages down our necks, paid the bill and headed for our hotel.

On the way back, we passed a line of pay phones. Scott decided to give Jackie a call. I said, "Its only 5 in the morning over there, I don't think it will go down too well, Scott." But it was too late; he had already begun to dial the number. The response as I had already predicted was a torrent of abuse from the other end of the phone, and 5 seconds later, we continued on our way with Scott mumbling under his breath, something I couldn't quite catch.

By now my body was screaming for sleep. I was absolutely knackered, we arrived nearly half an hour later back at our hotel only to find that the rooms were being cleaned and we would have to wait until the cleaners had finished before we could get back into our rooms.

I woke up in the lobby of the hotel at just after 1.00 with Scott dribbling and snoring on my shoulder. Nice! Beside us, not two feet away, lay both our suitcases. I jabbed Scott in the ribs and he woke at once complaining to me that I didn't need to punch him just to wake him up. I pointed at the suitcases. "Shit," he said, "What's all that about?" "I don't know," I replied, "Let's go and find out." We walked over to reception and tried our best to speak to the woman, who could speak as about as much English as we could speak German. We struggled along for about 5 minutes with no luck at all, but we had a bit of a break as someone walked passed, heard our dilemma and offered to help translate for us.

It turned out, on our arrival all we had managed to do was actually book our rooms for just one night, and now our rooms were occupied by some other people and there were no more vacant rooms for over two weeks. We thanked the chap who had helped us and wandered of into the street. Dragging our suitcases behind us, we knew there were no other cheap hotels in the locality, as we had tried nearly all of them just two nights ago. We opted to try a few up market hotels but after the third hotel, we decided to give it a miss as the cheapest one was nearly £80 a night, which would have taken nearly all our wages to pay for a room! In desperation, I called Paul and explained our problem to him. He said we could either stay on site in cabins or he knew of a flat for rent a little way out of town. As we had done the cabin thing before, I elected without consulting Scott to go for the flat, and arranged to meet Paul later in the afternoon to view it.

Paul met us at the Irish pub and after a quick beer and a chat; we followed him to a little place called Saatwinkle, just south of Spandau, about half an hours drive from the job to view the flat. It was in a boat yard which backed onto Lake Tegel. It was furnished and had three bedrooms, a huge lounge with a TV and a quite large kitchen, it was great. Paul spoke with the landlord and then to us. He told us it use to be his flat and because of that we got it at a reduced rate, just 600DM a month each. We said we would take it but we would have to find an ATM to pay the deposit and the months rent up front. The only downside of the situation was as Paul said; we would now have to register with the local police station.

After Paul helped us fill in the forms at the police station, which took over an hour and a half, we returned to our new digs to sort ourselves out and have a well earned sleep for a few hours. Scott woke up at about 9 O'clock and immediately started to complain that he was absolutely starving hungry!

On our arrival, we had noticed a steak house restaurant to the left hand side of the boat yard, so off we went across the boat yard and into the restaurant. It was a typical style German restaurant with boar heads and foxes, mounted on the walls but the guy who owned it, called Kalle made Scott and I feel very, very welcome. He spoke English with a heavy American accent and showed us to a table which was just in front of the main bar area.

As we were in a steak house, it seemed logical to order steak and chips. It was superb, I could see this place becoming a regular haunt for the pair of us, even though it was quite far away from the big lights of the city, it was also incredibly cheap indeed. The two steak and chips had cost us less than 6 pounds, and the large beers were only the equivalent of about £1.00!

Kalle came over and showed us a flier with the names of his restaurant on it and also something that read *TRAVASTIE NIGHT* on it, which happened to be that night! We didn't understand what he was going on about, so we just smiled at him and ordered another two beers. An hour later we understood exactly what a travastie night was because the door suddenly burst open and in walked 6 transvestites all dressed in stockings and suspenders, with high heel boots and mini skirts to match! The music started from somewhere behind the bar and the show began.

The impromptu stage just happened to be the area between Scott and I and the bar. The transvestites were dancing and miming to the music and gyrating up and down not more than six feet in front of Scott and me! The rest of the customers in the restaurant were clapping and cheering, the more they clapped and cheered, the more the transvestites gyrated and cavorted about. Both Scott and I were totally gob smacked; neither of us had ever seen anything quite like this in our lives before. The music stopped and one of the transvestites began a magic show, which as it happened, was very professional with rabbits in hats and pigeons popping up all over the place. He, she or it was actually good and kept the audience completely spellbound for nearly half an hour or so.

The next act started and I knew at once it was one of those acts that was going to require some audience participation, and as Scott and I had rather long hair, I knew without a doubt we were going to be singled out to take part in someway shape of form. Because of our long hair, they may have thought that Scott and I may have been from the same brotherhood of transvestites!

I said to Scott, "You know who's going to get picked out for this act, don't you?" "Yes," he replied, "Either you or me mate, I think." I said to Scott I was going to go to the toilet. "Chicken," he said. But as I stood up to go, the trannie grabbed my arm and dragged me up in front of everyone. Oh shit! I thought. I don't need this; I really don't need this at all! He opened a packet of cigarettes and placed one between each of my fingers and one in my mouth, which he motioned for me to light up. He grabbed both my hands and positioned them palms down and cigarettes up, outstretched in front of me. I looked up and saw Scott grinning like a little kid in front of me.

I heard the whips cracking before I actually saw them. Oh god, I thought, I hope this bloody idiot knows what he's doing. The music began, it was Rawhide, and he, she…it went for it with a very nasty looking whip in each hand. They were cracking loudly around my head and every so often he would twirl around and crack out a cigarette in one of my hands. At least he was quite accurate I thought. I now had four cigarettes burning slowly down in my left hand and one still in my mouth. I could see Scott, who by now was almost in tears with laughter. You bastard, I thought. The trannie continued to dance and twirl around me, crack and out went the last cigarette in my left hand. Now all that was left was the one in my mouth, which I had noticed was less than an inch long! The music was building up to the crescendo and as the word Rawhide was sung, he spun around and cracked the whip in the direction of the cigarette in my mouth. I head the whip crack and still saw the cigarette dangling out of my mouth. You missed, I thought to myself. Yeah, he missed the cigarette alright and had clipped me with the whip just under my chin.

It was only a small cut, about two centimetres long, but it had cut me quite deeply and two or three seconds later it began pouring with blood down the front of my shirt and on to the floor in front of me! I've never minded women fussing over me when I've hurt myself, but I took a very dim view to three blokes masquerading as women, fussing over me especially as one of them looked like a double of Morticia from the Adams family. Five minutes later I was back in my seat, all patched up with a huge plaster on my chin. The show went on but now every two minutes or so, one of the trannies would blow me a kiss, or wave at me just to ensure I was still breathing I think. But Scott and everyone else there that night fount it absolutely hilarious and the more they all laughed, the more kisses were blown in my direction.

At last the finale began and I couldn't believe it. The music began and they all stood in a line directly in front of Scott and me and started to strip! No, no, don't do it, I thought, and I turned to Scott who was also pulling faces and I said to him, "This is unbelievable, I just hope they don't go all the way." "I'll be sick if they do, really sick," said Scott. Thank god, they got down to their leather underwear and stopped. "Bloody hell, that was close," said Scott. "Yeah," I replied, "Well close."

The stage cleared and the music returned to traditional Germany military marching music and people returned to their seats, their meals and drinks. Kalle came over to see how my chin was, and ten seconds later I was mobbed by the six trannies, now all dressed in leather mini skirts, knee length boots, along with enough make up to float a ship. They were all flapping around me, lifting my chin up, making clucking noises and stroking my hair, and patting me on the back. Kalle translated for the guy who had cut me with the whip and he insisted on buying me yet another beer by way of an apology. The next thing we knew, the trannies had dragged a table and chairs next to ours and we spent the rest of the evening surrounded by the trannies, they would not leave me alone all night long, and kept buying beers for Scott and me every time we finished one.

Funnily enough, we had a great evening. The best part was that with Kalle now sitting with us translating, we were able to talk to the trannies, and the evening absolutely flew past. By now everyone was totally bladdered. We had been on the beer at least 7 hours again. At two O'clock we asked Kalle for our bill, but he said the trannies had picked it up for us. We thanked them and they asked us if we were coming next Saturday night to see their new act. We both agreed and stumbled off in a drunken stupor back to our flat.

German beer contains no preservatives, no colourings and no chemicals whatsoever, so when I woke Sunday morning with a blinding hangover, I was a bit perplexed as to why, until Scott came in and said, "I'm not drinking that schnapps crap again, my head feels like someone's playing a tune in there with a huge hammer!" "Me too," I said, "I feel awful."

We thought we would go for a walk to clear the cobwebs and to get some fresh air. To the right hand side of the boat yard was a beach nearly two kilometres long with lovely white sand. It looked more like a seaside resort, it was very pretty. On the beach was a take away imbis selling ice creams and hot food. It was only ten in the morning but it was already open for business, so we took our shoes and socks off and walked across the already hot sand to get something to eat and drink. But yet again, the choice was fairly limited to sausages or sausages or sausages. So, we had a sausage each.

We wandered off in the other direction, past the boat yard and into the woods which were full of small wooden chalet type bungalows, with German families already out soaking up the hot August sun. We later learned these were summer weekend houses, which the Germans used on the weekends to get away from the hustle and bustle of city life. By chance some ten minutes later, we came across a payphone which gave us the opportunity to call home. Scott dialled and talked to Jackie and the kids for a few minutes before passing the phone to me. I was expecting Louise to be on the other end, but it was still Jackie. "Hi Jackie," I said, "How are you getting on, sweetheart?" "Fine," she said, and then told me that Louise had moved back into my house and thought it may be a good idea to give her a call. I thanked her and hung up and immediately dialled my own number. Louise answered on the first ring. I didn't give her even time to say hello and jumped straight down her throat. "What the hell are you doing back in the house?" I said, "There's a family moving in at the end of the month, I can't afford for you to be in the house until I've paid all our debts off." She hung up on me. I dialled again and got the engaged signal. "Christ," I said to Scott, "What the hell is she up to?" "Don't know," said Scott. I tried to dial again and still got the engaged signal. I called Jackie back and asked her to pop around to my house and get Louise to answer the phone. Ten minutes later I called again and she picked the phone up at last. "What's going on?" I asked. "I can't stay there, it's too loud," she said. I thought, bloody hell, you want to hear the noise you make; I didn't say it for fear of her hanging up again! "Well, I can't afford for you to stay in the house until we've paid all our debts off, and on top of that, there's a family moving in and I've signed the contract with them, so you've got no choice but to go to Scott and Jackie's house," I said. "Ok, I'll move back in," she said. "Thank god for that," I said. She asked how things were going and we chatted for another few minutes but all of a sudden I ran out of change and the phone went dead.

Scott and I decided to do a dry run to the building site that afternoon just to see how long it would take us to get there, because we didn't want to be late on our first day at work on a new job. It only took us twenty five minutes which wasn't bad at all. We filled up with diesel and drove back to the boat yard and spent a very relaxing afternoon sitting in Kalle's steak house slowly, and very slowly drinking a few beers and watching people coming and going in to the restaurant and the boat yard.

An early night was on the cards, so we watched a bit of TV but the only channel in English was MTV so we watched a bit of Beavis and

Butthead and hit the sack.

Monday arrived completely hangover free, which was quite nice and at 6.15 we jumped in the van and made our way to work. The other lads were waiting outside to get in. We parked up and the day began. Simon walked us round and found Scott and I a wall to demolish. The Germans supplied all the power tools and off we went. The building was over 150 years old and the dust absolutely stank to high heaven. After ten minutes we could hardly see two feet in front of our faces and stopped to let it settle a bit. In the pile of rubble was a small metal box about a foot square. I picked it up and shook it; there was something inside rattling around. I got a kango and smashed it open. Inside was a bunch of keys. Scott began to laugh all that effort to open it and the keys were on the inside. "What a waste of time," he said.

I threw the keys into my toolbox and we continued to knock down the wall. By breakfast time we had managed to knock the whole wall down and were just beginning to chuck it into a skip, when Simon called tea up. We went with Simon and Ray to a small bakers, not more than two hundred metres up the street and ordered a breakfast of egg sandwiches and coffee, with the help of Simon doing the ordering for us. It was quite embarrassing not being able to even order a cup of coffee and I made my mind up right then to make an effort somehow to learn a bit of German, to enable me to get by.

I mentioned to Simon about the keys I had found and he said to show them to him when we got back to the site after breakfast. Twenty minutes later we were back at work. I showed Simon the keys and he said to go to a jeweller and get them assayed after work. "Why?" I asked. "They are probably gold," he said, "The Jews melted down all their gold and made it into household items, like keys and door latches in order to stop the Germans confiscating it for their own use and as this building is an old Jewish slaughter house, I would suspect your keys may well be solid gold!" "Bloody hell," I said, they were quite heavy as well and stuffed them into my pocket. After work we walked up and down the streets looking for a goldsmith or jeweller shop. We found one after about half an hour and went in. I handed the man behind the counter the keys, not a word had been spoken. He disappeared into the back of the shop and returned less than two minutes later and simply handed me two one thousand DM notes and rattle off something in German at us. I looked at Scott, his mouth was hanging open, "That's about £800," he said. "Yes, I know," I replied and we walked out of the shop. "Look at that," I said, "We've only been in Germany five days and we've got £800 already." I couldn't believe our luck.

We went into an electrical shop and bought ourselves a video player, some videos, a toaster, a kettle, and a hand held computer game to keep us amused. As we walked back clutching our new toys, we watched as our van went past us being towed by a big tow truck, with the front wheels off the ground. "Oh shit," I said, "Now what do we do?" "Bloody hell," said Scott and began whistling at the driver trying to attract his attention, but it was too late, he was already disappearing around the corner.

I could tell by the tone of Paul's voice that he wasn't too amused by our problem. He suggested we went to the nearest police station to make enquiries as to the where abouts of our van. After asking half a dozen people or so, we at last came to the local plod shop and still clutching our boxes went inside. "This is going to be a bit complicated I think Scott," I said. We walked up to the front desk and asked the policeman behind it if anyone here could speak any English. "A little," he replied. "Good," I said, "We have had our van towed away from the street just around the corner, and would like to know how we go about getting it back." "Passport and driving license," he said." "Both in the van," I replied. "Follow me please," he said and off we went through the police station and out into a compound behind it. Sure enough there was our van parked in the corner. I opened the van and got the paperwork out, along with our passports and licenses. We trundled back into the police station and the lecture began. "You no park in bus lane," he said. "Oops, sorry," I said, "We didn't know it was a bus lane." "You pay me now," he said. "Ok, how much?" I replied. He looked through a chart on the wall and promptly said 300DM. We stumped up the money and he gave us a piece of paper with a stamp and his signature on it, and pointed to the compound. "You go," he said. We chucked all our stuff in the van and drove to the gate. Scott handed the man in the booth the piece of paper and up went the barrier and off we went. "Won't park there again," said Scott with a grin on his face. "Never mind, at least we had the money to get our van back!" I said.

We spent the rest of the week at work scouring the site for more boxes in walls and checking all of the door handles and latches, hoping to find another piece of gold, but unfortunately we found nothing at all. Saturday arrived and so did Paul with our first pay check of 1750DM because we had only worked five days and the pay week went from Saturday to Friday. Nonetheless, we were well chuffed, it was the equivalent of nearly £700 at the present exchange rate, and it was all cash which was even better. Smiles all round.

Simon had told us of a cheap way of sending cash back to England with an American company called Western Union, and it took less than two minutes to fill out the forms and was very simple. The commission you paid was also quite reasonable as well. As soon as we had sent the money, we phoned the girls and told them how to go about picking it up in England. Louise was in a better mood as she had now finished her training and had opted to fluctuate between the various world wide stock exchanges, which meant working different shifts at silly hours during the night, but she had been offered a very good financial package and was full of herself. It also meant she would be able to pay off her student loan now an awful lot quicker than I or she had previously thought which as she said, would mean I would now need to spend less time in Germany, and we could also discharge all our debts more quickly. Things were looking up again, which cheered me up no end.

Scott got off the phone and I knew by the stupid grin on his face, even before he opened his mouth what had happened. "She's pregnant again," I said. "Yep," said Scott "Lets celebrate." My liver really needed a holiday, but there was no way Scott would let me abstain from drinking so we parked up outside our flat and hit Kalle's steak house with a vengeance. We sat out in the beer garden in the lovely hot evening sun and got completely trollied. At some time after nine O'clock we went back inside and as we walked in, the trannies walked in behind us. "Oh no, not again," I said. Scott just grinned at me.

We sat at a table far enough away as to not get dragged into the proceedings again and ordered something to eat. We watched the act now from a safe distance, but I needn't have worried as this week they were all riding uni-cycles and juggling oranges and lemons. It was hilarious. The whole restaurant was packed out and everyone was almost crying with laughter at the antics of the trannies!

I challenge any bloke whose wife or girlfriend is not with them to tell them they have had enough to drink and its time to go home to be able to, after loads of drinks, make that decision for themselves. It's impossible, I guarantee it! But after losing the ability to focus and also having a bit of trouble with the walking and balance thing, we at last made up our minds to go home and stumbled off yet again in the direction of our flat.

August rolled into September, but the weather remained absolutely beautiful, hot and cloud free. The weeks were flying by, we thought in order to save a bit more money we would restrict our drinking to Saturday nights and Sundays only, and not to go drinking every day of the week until some hideous time in the morning and end up feeling like shit all the following day! The days were beginning to get noticeably shorter now but the evenings were still very, very warm. We bought some fishing rods from our land lord and began to sit on the beach next to the boat yard in the warm evening sun and do some serious fishing. It was brilliant, both Scott and I loved fishing, plus it was also a great way of keeping us out of the pubs during the week, which also meant being hangover free during the working week, so it was a good bonus and fantastic way of saving even more money. After all, the whole idea of coming to Germany was actually to make money and get us out of financial trouble and not sit in pubs 24/7 drinking the money away! We were sending an average of between £5-600 home every week now, which left us both enough to pay our rent, buy food and diesel for the van and also left a bit over for Saturday night and Sundays in the pub. We ate out every evening because it was cheaper than trying to cook at home and to be quite honest; Scott and I were about as good at cooking as my mother is at driving a car! So, we went for the soft option and ate mostly at Kalle's steak house which suited us fine.

By the end of September, I had managed to pay off one credit card completely, which cheered me up no end, and according to Louise, I was now only two months in areas with the mortgage, which was great news but I still had five more credit cards to deal with. Even so, I could now at last begin to see the light at the end of the tunnel! Two weeks later our birthdays arrived, and we made the very bad mistake of telling some of the Polish labourers that we had come to know quite well on our site, who insisted that after work both Scott and I were to join them behind their cabins on the site for a barbeque and a few drinks to celebrate. We didn't really want to but decided it would be very rude not to accept and we promised each other that we would only have a couple of drinks as we had yet still to drive home.

The Polish were issued on application to the German government a work permit to work in Germany for three months in any twelve month period. They did this purely and simply to earn good money from the German construction companies. After talking to them we found their average wage in Poland was between £12-15 a week and the Germans would pay them, on average, about the same £12-15 but a day. The tight gits, I thought! But the Polish loved it; they went home after their three month stint and in their eyes absolutely loaded.

Scott and I felt very sorry for them and hoped they had no gone to too much trouble and expense on this barbeque. We needn't have worried at all because as we walked around the back of their cabins after work, the barbeque was full of what looked suspiciously like road kill and the bottles of drink were in clear bottles with no labels on them at all! I looked at Scott and raised an eyebrow at him. He said, "We agreed to come mate, the least we can do is have a quick bite to eat and a couple of drinks, then we can make our excuses and shoot off home." "Ok," I said, "But let's make it no more than a couple?" "Ok," said Scott.

A steaming hot plate of road kill was thrust into each of our hands, along with a half pint glass of this clear liquid topped up with coke. I took a sip and was almost instantly sick. I looked over to Scott; he was gurning back at me. "Let's just down it," he said and added, "Perhaps it's their national drink, and we better not offend them." So down it went, god it tasted bloody awful, and to our horror, they then thrust another full glass into each of our hands and motioned to us to repeat the process. I ate a piece of my road kill in an attempt to get the taste out of my mouth, but as I began chewing, whatever they had marinated the meat in was hotter than chillies so I had to gulp down another mouthful of the awful liquid. As soon as I had managed to stop coughing I said to Scott, while still gasping for breath, "Don't eat the meat mate, its awful." But it was too late, he had already bitten off a huge chunk and a few seconds after he began chewing it, began coughing and spluttering, his face went a deep crimson colour, and he then gulped down a couple of mouthfuls of the foul liquid.

While all eyes were focused on Scott and his coughing fit, I managed to launch my piece of meat straight over the fence and into the property next door. There was absolutely no way on this earth I could be tempted to eat another piece of whatever it was, and it certainly wasn't beef, pork, or anything even remotely similar! Scott was still bent over double coughing and making all sorts of funny noises but at last after nearly five minutes, he eventually regained his composure. But even then his eyes were still watering and he was also still very, very red in the face. It wasn't even something that you could laugh about, Scott downed the rest of his drink in one go, and immediately was given another full one to replace it.

Now I knew it would be me that was going to be driving home, and managed to pour the rest of my drink into a storm drain, while no one was watching me. Scott by now had fully recovered and walked up to me and said, "I think its time to go home, mate." "Good idea," I said, "Let's make some excuse and head for home." We thanked the Poles and beat a hasty retreat to the van and made our getaway without too much trouble. We hadn't gone far when I had to stop the van and throw up on the side of the road. Five minutes later, Scott followed suit and by the time we got home I think we had both chucked up at least four or five times each. We both felt really ill and as soon as we got home, went straight to bed. It was only 7.30 in the evening and through the night we managed between us to chuck up another two or three times at least.

The following morning we still felt awful and decided to take the day off work and stay at home in an attempt to recover from whatever it was we had eaten and drunk the night before! By midday I felt well enough to walk up to the payphone and I called Paul to apologise for not making it into work. I told him what had happened the previous evening. "You were both lucky you didn't end up in hospital having your stomachs pumped," he said. "What do you mean?" I asked. "They are well known for drinking surgical spirit as it only costs 20p a bottle," he said. "Oh my god," I replied, "That stuff could kill you, bloody hell, that's all I need!" I was going to ask him what he thought the meat might have been, but as my stomach was still feeling quite delicate, I decided against it and instead wandered back towards our flat wondering how many Poles had managed to kill themselves by drinking surgical spirit. The stupid bloody idiots.

When I got back to the flat, Scott was mobile but not functioning very well and he was also looking a bit green still. I told him what Paul had said to me and he went ballistic. "I'll bloody kill those arseholes on Monday," he said, "That's bang out of order doing that to us, especially knowing what it was and what it could do to your intestines. I'm going to kill them," he repeated.

We spent the rest of the day flat out on the settees watching the videos we had bought only to find they were all in German, nonetheless it was something to watch but I found it quite hard to get my head around, watching Open All Hours with David Jason and Ronny Barker speaking in German. It wasn't until nearly eight O'clock that evening that we managed to peel ourselves off of the settees and make our way down to Kalle's to get something to eat, and as we approached the door, I noticed the poster advertising the Travestie show for that evening. Scott just groaned and said, "I can't cope with those idiots tonight," but we needed to get something to eat and also get some more fluids into our bodies. So in we went and found a table at the back and out of the way! The evening passed without any problems and we actually got back to the flat before 10.30 and went back to bed.

Our idea on Sunday was to spend it fishing on the beach, but as we walked out the gate with our fishing gear and headed towards the beach, I noticed our van. There were no wheels on it, some extremely kind person had jacked it up on bricks and removed all the wheels and on inspection had left the wheel nuts stacked tidily by each axle. "For Christ's sake," I said, "Can't anything in this country just be normal?" Scott went into total meltdown and swore steadily for over five minutes. "This is going to cost a fortune," he eventually said when he had stopped swearing. "Well there's nothing we can do on a Sunday," I said, "We may as well just go fishing and try to enjoy it and get a quote for new tyres and wheels tomorrow," I added.

Poor Paul made the phone calls for us on the Monday and by that evening we had brand new wheels and tyres, plus some locking wheel nuts, but the downside was it had cost us nearly £900 for the privilege and it wasn't an expense we had bargained for at all, plus the fact we had had a day off work as well which meant we had also lost another £130 each to boot!

We had now been in Germany the best part of three months and we made our minds up to go home for a few days. The girls and Scott's four kids met us at the airport and after we got them all strapped into the camper, made our way back home to what we hoped would be normal food and at last a bit of English TV. The four days disappeared in the blink of an eye and the next thing we knew we were on our way back to Heathrow airport. It didn't seem fair, it was so nice being back at home but the money we were earning in Germany was the only way we were going to be able to maintain our houses and mortgages. The recession was now in full swing at home and in the short time we had been at home, had been able to talk to various friends and building companies who were by now all struggling quite badly financially. Scott and I both knew that Germany was realistically the only option, until such time as the recession ended or we became able to earn a living wage again in England.

Scott's kids were not too happy about their daddy going away again and as we walked towards departures, were hanging off his shirt in a vain attempt to stop him going. It was heart wrenching but we had to go, we had no option. We had a last cuddle with the girls and went off through departures without looking back.

The following week on the 9th of November, the Berlin wall came down and Germany went into total party mode. The whole place was going absolutely mental; the TV was full of pictures of the East Germans crossing the wall which had kept them divided from the west since 1961. Everyone almost stopped going to work and spent their time in pubs and the streets celebrating the demise of communism. It was crazy, everywhere we went people were drinking and celebrating. The German press were having a field day; it was the biggest thing of that decade. The papers were full of pictures of families being reunited and before and after pictures of towns and cities not seen for decades.

The next few weeks, we saw military trucks, tanks and personal carriers being driven around, obviously back to Russia or to a wrecking yard, maybe to be crushed or destroyed. The West Germans were now going into the old east to explore and in some cases try to get their old family homes and land back somehow from the now newly reunited East Germany.

World attention was now focused on Germany and in particular Berlin itself. TV crews from all over the world were flooding into Berlin and filming everything from houses to cars, the wall itself and the East German people themselves. You could not even walk down the street without seeing satellite dishes hanging off the side of big panel vans and camera crews running around all over the place, like headless chickens filming anything and everything that moved!

Military personnel were also being repatriated and the TV and press were reporting on the mass exodus of the occupying troops, going back home to their various own countries.

Scott and I also spent our day off the following Sunday exploring the former East Germany. It was an eye opener; the roads were more like dirt tracks and the houses looked as if they hadn't been looked after at all for years, not even a coat of paint or anything. We wandered around a small suburb not more than twenty kilometres from where we were living and we could still see bullet holes in the walls of buildings and bomb damage that hadn't been repaired since the Second World War had finished, some fifty four years previously. We were gob smacked, and decided that we would buy a camera with our next week's wages in order to get some pictures of what I can only describe as probably the most interesting thing I had ever seen in my life, before it disappeared forever!

The roads were now also full of East German cars called Trabants; they were very small cars with a two stroke engine and were stinking the place out with the clouds of smog that followed in their wake. The shell of the cars were made of something very similar to fibreglass but it wasn't, it was more like a resin bonded paper or something fairly similar. The cars themselves were capable of going about 50mph absolutely flat out and because the East Germans were not use to the fact that a BMW or Mercedes could go at least twice as fast or if not more, were pulling out in front of BMWs and faster cars on duel carriageways and motorways, causing horrendous accidents all over the place. Everywhere Scott and I drove, we would see Trabants dumped on the side of the roads nearly reduced to their component parts by the impact of the faster cars; there was almost an epidemic of accidents in the first month after the wall came down and I wondered how the occupants of these comical little cars had faired in these accidents. Not very well I expected.

The weather had suddenly and without warning, turned from ten or twelve degrees Celsius and dropped to something horrible and very, very, minus degrees. I can tolerate any kind of heat and in fact I quite enjoy it, but the cold is something else. I detest it. There is nothing worse in this world than being cold and freezing to the bone, and to make it even worse, we had now started the face work on the outside of the building and had to cut some of the bricks with a bench cutter. This meant getting covered in cold water every time you cut a brick as the blade was water cooled. We were freezing to death everyday now and also spending a large part of the day soaking wet from the cutter. Lovely!

The next three cold and wet weeks dragged by very slowly, but at last it was the week before Christmas and we headed to the airport and off home for ten days of well earned holiday, and hopefully some proper Christmas dinner too! Jackie and her bump, along with Louise, met us at the airport and Scott drove us back home. We had our first English pint in the Kings Arms and also a meal in the village to celebrate the fact we could now again eat English food. It was fantastic to be back at home again; I was looking forward to having some quality time at home, without having to get up at 5.00 in the morning and go to work. Jackie and Louise had prepared Christmas down to a tee; it was a great time, with Scott's four kids making the most of their presents, or more to the point, enjoying playing with the packing that the gifts came in and making an absolute total mess all around the house.

On Boxing Day, Louise and I left Scott and Jackie at home with the brats and went round to see my parents for the day. It was a typically normal day there; my dad was stuck in front of the TV as usual watching absolutely anything and flicking through the channels every five minutes looking for something more interesting to watch. My mother was predictably stuck in a book reading some love triangle story or something equally as boring. We stayed for most of the day and just before six O'clock, said our goodbyes and headed for the Kings Arms to meet up with Scott and the tribe.

The rest of the week went by far too quickly for my liking and here we were again, standing in front of departures saying our goodbyes yet again. Louise now had another three weeks holiday to take and we had arranged for the two girls and the kids to come over in six to eight weeks time to stay in the flat with us and have a short break in Germany, and also a good look around Berlin and the shops!

As Scott and I flew into Tegel airport, we noticed everywhere was covered with a light dusting of snow; it looked quite picturesque, but as we walked from the plane it was absolutely bloody freezing, at least minus twenty degrees! "Bloody hell," said Scott, "That's cold."

Customs, as per usual, played their same tricks on Scott and I but this time we had no baggage at all, not even hand luggage, but even so we were asked a lot of stupid questions, including 'why haven't you got any luggage with you?' You just can't win with these people and it just further proved to me that it's the way you dress, or in our case, the length of your hair, that makes you an instant threat to security and also immediately a drug dealer because of the way you look. Never mind. After nearly ten minutes of why this and why that, we were eventually allowed to continue on our way. We got back to our flat about forty minutes later. There were people everywhere and on closer inspection, we saw the lake had totally frozen over. There were people walking on it and also, believe it or not, driving cars across it!

We went to Kalle's for a coffee; he wished us a happy new year and asked if we were coming to the party that night. "What party?" asked Scott? "The party on the lake," replied Kalle. "Sounds like fun," I said. 7.30 That evening Scott and I walked from our flat, through the boat yard and out into the ice. It was well over three feet thick and didn't even make a noise when you walked on it. Around all the big boats moored in the water, were sprinkler systems that agitated the water so the ice remained about two feet away from the hull of the boats. By standing next to this you could see how thick the ice was.

In the distance, some two hundred metres away, we could see a big fire burning. We headed for it and presumed the party must be on one of the small islands dotted all over the lake. But as we approached, the fire was actually blazing on the ice itself. "Unbelievable," I said to Scott, "Its going to melt the ice don't you think?" As we got closer, we could see a beer tent erected on the ice. Kalle was standing next to it with a huge barbeque cooking steaks and kebabs. He was dressed in a clowns outfit and looked like he was enjoying himself. There were maybe eighty to a hundred people standing around the fire to keep warm because by now, it was below minus twenty six degrees. We had seen a thermometer in the boat yard and couldn't believe how cold it was. Kalle saw us and motioned for us to come over. He gave us a plate of kebabs and told us to get a beer from the beer tent; we retreated to the fire because as you walked away from it you just froze.

About an hour later, the transvestites turned up all dressed in full length fur coats and high heal shoes, wigs and makeup everywhere, and tottered around the ice looking like they might fall over at any second. But at least it was a social visit tonight and not one of their shows, thank god.

At ten O'clock there were fireworks and even the Germans were *oohing* and *aarhing* every time they went off. It was mostly the trannies doing most of the *oohing* and *aarhing*, but even so it was a good display and had only cost us 20DM each by the end of the evening, which was good value for money in anyone's books! We had been up since 4am that morning, so we decided to hit the sack and get some sleep. We waved goodbye to Kalle and the trannies and nearly died of hypothermia walking back to our flat.

I woke Sunday morning and looked out the window. It was blue sky and brilliant sunshine, and the whole world and their wives, dogs, kids and grandparents were wandering around on the ice outside. I could see ice yachts flying up and down at incredible speeds, there was also a game of ice hockey in progress just in front of the boats. It looked like fun and brought back memories of Richmond ice rink, and me and Scott behaving mostly badly! After a quick breakfast, we went outside, wrapped up like Eskimos to join the rest of the people wandering about.

It was absolutely freezing, it made your nose hurt like hell just breathing. In the distance we could see the small town of Tegel and as the crow flies, it was about five kilometres away. We decided to walk there as we had never been there before. We headed off in that direction across the ice avoiding on the way the ice yachts and the odd car, which were tearing around at breakneck speeds and scaring the living daylights out of people in the process.

We arrived in Tegel nearly an hour later and found a rather nice French style bar called Papillion in to warm up and have a beer or six! My hands were burning as they began to warm up. It was very reminiscent of the feeling I use to have riding my motorbike and also still as painful. The rest of the afternoon was devoted to the beer god, Warsteiner, who came in a close second to the only other beer god, Stella, and at 4pm we paid our bill as we knew it would be getting dark before 5.30 and we had an hours walk in front of us, and also with beer now fuelling the process, it would probably more than likely take nearer to an hour and a half to get back to the flat across the ice.

We returned to work the next morning and Paul wished us a happy New Year and immediately asked us if we were prepared to go to a job in a town called Frankfurt Oder on the Polish border. "What about our accommodation?" I asked. "Not a problem," said Paul, "There's accommodation supplied for free." "Not cabins," said Scott, "We're not doing cabins especially now it's so cold." "No," said Paul, "Its hotel accommodation paid for by the construction company, plus you will be earning a bit more money." he added. "How much more then?" I asked. "At least another 650DM a week" said Paul, "If not more." We were sold, and Paul gave us the day off to pack and two hours later we were following him up the motorway, just north east of Berlin.

We drove for just under an hour, about sixty miles in total, until we arrived in Frankfurt Oder, a very grey and depressing looking town on the River Oder, which was also the border between Germany and Poland, and pulled into a small building site. Simon and Ray were already there and were beavering away building a cellar, some twenty metres square. As we approached they came up to meet us and Paul went through the drawings with us, and half an hour later Paul was on his way and left us to it. The hotel was directly opposite the site and Simon came in with us to do all the necessary translating. We dumped out bags in a room that we were going to have to share, and trotted off back over to the site to have a proper chat with Simon and Ray about the job.

Simon said we would only be on the job about two and a half to three weeks long, as we only had to build the external walls, and as there were now four of us on the job, it wouldn't take too long at all. We obviously would have a day or twos wait, while the chippies cast each of the two floors, but even so, he forecast no more than three weeks in total to finish.

Scott and I grabbed our tools from the van and jumped in with Simon and Ray. The blocks were absolutely huge things about 900mm x 360mm x 360mm and were not bonded together the traditional way with sand and cement mortar, but with a glue which was similar in consistency to a wet plaster mix and you couldn't use a trowel but used what I can only describe as a big ladle with serrated teeth to give the bed some volume and to allow the blocks to be moved around. The system was extremely good and also very quick indeed.

By Friday afternoon we had finished the cellar and cut the cellar windows in, two on each flank. The Germans were already tanking the outside walls to make them waterproof and as we walked away they began the shuttering for the concrete slab, which Simon said they would be pouring over the weekend. We now had two and a half days to kill so we all went back to the hotel, showered and changed and between the four of us, made our minds up to go across the border and into Poland to explore a country that none of us had ever been to but had heard quite a lot about from the various different Polish labourers we had talked to, or been working with over the past months.

We took Ray's car only because it had four seats as oppose to our van which only had three, and drove over the River Oder Bridge and into Poland itself. Customs just waved us through without stopping the car. This was a brand new experience for me and I began to laugh, Scott realised why I was laughing and before long we were in fits of laughter again. Simon and Ray just stared at us wondering what the hell it was that was so funny, but they both saw the funny side once we had explained the reason for our mirth!

The first thing we noticed on entering Poland was the amount of women, standing on the side of the roads in very short mini skirts and skimpy tops, and as it was still something very horribly minus degrees, wondered what in gods name they were doing freezing to death on the side of the roads until Simon said they were prostitutes touting for business. But even so, they must have been absolutely freezing.

We drove through two or three small; one horse towns and about an hour later came to a fairly big town. We couldn't even read the name of the town, let alone pronounce it. But it had hotels and shops in abundance, so we elected to stop and have a good look round. The first place we found was a hypermarket the size of an aircraft hanger. Ray parked up and we all tramped inside to see exactly what they had for sale.

It was an Aladdin's cave and sold almost anything you could think of Scott and I walked around for over an hour. By now we had lost both Simon and Ray and as the place was so huge, we made our way to the checkouts hoping to eventually bump into them again. They were both already there waiting for us. Ray had a carrier bag in his hand, and Scott asked him what he had bought. He opened the bag and pulled out a machine pistol! "Bloody hell," said Scott and I simultaneously. "It's only a replica," said Ray, "But it looks brilliant, doesn't it?" he said. Bloody nutter, I thought.

We drove back into town and searched for a hotel. Ten minutes later we had booked into a four star hotel. It was only £2.50 a night with a breakfast included in the price, unbelievably cheap, but quite normal in Poland. None of us had thought to bring a change of clothes or toiletries with us. Dirty pigs, I hear you say!

We changed some German Deutsch marks into Polish Zlotys, and for the first, and I expect the last time in my life, I became a millionaire instantly. I had changed 200DM and in return had almost enough paper money to fill a standard size carrier bag full with it!

We walked into the restaurant and found ourselves a table and sat down. The waiter arrived and as he spoke German, as well as Polish, Simon ordered everyone's meal for them, and also four enormous Polish beers. We had all ordered the same meal, steak and chips. Then one of the weirdest things I've ever seen in my life happened. The waiter returned with a huge plate, and on the plate was our four steaks, and stacked next to them a huge pile of chips and a small pot of peas. From a cabinet in the corner of the restaurant he pulled out a set of kitchen scales, and bought them to the table. He then got four dinner plates out and began to weigh the steaks in front of us. Each time he put a steak on the scales, he then showed us exactly how much it weighted and put it on a plate. We sat there wondering what the hell was going on, looking at each other and trying not to laugh out loud.

The process continued with both the potato chips and also the peas. Now all four plates were full of uncooked food. He then picked up the four plates and disappeared into the kitchen. The door shut behind him and we all began to howl with laughter. As it happened, the meal was very good indeed, and the total bill for the meal including eight large beers and also a tip was only the equivalent of £10. We couldn't believe how cheap this place was!

We wandered outside and up and down a few streets until we came to what looked like a pub, and dived in. The beer was a bit sour tasting but only about 15p a pint, so we made absolute pigs of ourselves for the rest of the afternoon and into the evening. About ten O'clock, the pub started filling up with the locals, who all seemed to have been to the same clothes outlet. Everything they were wearing was black, from trousers to shirts and jackets; all black. The women and younger girls were all wearing pencil skirts and flowery blouses, very 70's. It was obvious that fashion as we knew it had not been embraced by the Polish yet! Then the disco started, and I nearly spat my beer into Scott's face. 'Tie a yellow ribbon round the old oak tree' began thumping out at about a hundred and fifty decibels, and Scott and I just broke down into a fit of the giggles yet again.

We returned to our hotel at gone 1.30 and between the four of us, we had managed to spend the huge sum of £13 the whole day and evening. Sunday after breakfast, we spend the day wandering around the town looking at old buildings and historic churches and also sampled a few more of the local pubs. Late afternoon, we checked out of the hotel and made our way back towards Frankfurt Oder, stopping on the way again at the hypermarket to buy cigarettes and booze to take back to Germany.

We pulled out of the hypermarket and as we did so, Ray's car began to make some very strange noises. First it began clonking quite loudly and then it began overheating. We limped our way back down the road and passed a sign post saying ninety kilometres to the border. Ray was now talking to the old Granada, trying to coax it along a bit but not more than six kilometres down the road it just stopped completely, with steam pouring out from under the bonnet.

We got out of the car and between us managed to push the old tank off the road and on to the grass verge. Less than two minutes later, the girls who were standing along the street started arriving in twos and threes asking us if we wanted to do some business with them. Ray had bought the old Granada about a month previously for £250 and said he wasn't bothered about repairing it, but even so we still now had a major problem. We were over a hundred kilometres from the building site in Germany, we had no car, it was also below minus twenty degrees and we had no telephone and had not even passed one that we could remember.

Simon asked one of the Polish prostitutes if she could phone for a taxi for us and after parting with the equivalent of £10, one of them called on our behalf on her mobile. She said to Simon it would be at least one and a half hours before it would get to us. We got back in Ray's old car in an attempt to keep warm. Ray kept trying to start the car but it was completely dead. We sat for half an hour before Ray remembered we had a couple of crates of beer in the boot of the car, and so we began to drink it while we waited for the taxi to arrive. An hour passed and there was no sign of the taxi. We carried on drinking and chatting in the car. After another hour still nothing and Simon wandered up the road to find the girl with the mobile phone to see if she could phone again or at least get a time when the taxi would arrive. "Another hour," said Simon as he jumped back in the car. "Bloody hell, we'll be pissed or dead by then," said Ray. It was nearly ten O'clock and it was freezing, freezing cold.

At last at 11.15 the taxi arrived and we all jumped into it as quickly as we could. I was sure we were in the first stages of frost bite by now, my lips were numb and Scott was complaining that his fingers were killing him. Obviously all the alcohol hadn't helped the situation at all. Simon told the taxi driver where we wanted to go and off we went, Simon in the front, and Scott, Ray and I slumped in the back of the cab fast asleep in seconds. At three am the following morning, I woke up with a start; we were still in the taxi. I looked at the next sign post on the motorway and saw to my horror a kilometre sign saying *Frankfurt Main 293km.* I shook Simon awake and told him what I had just seen on the motorway sign. "Oh shit," said Simon and began quickly talking to the taxi driver. By now everyone was awake wondering what the hell was going on. What had actually happened was the cab driver had though we wanted to go to Frankfurt Main, which was between six hundred and seven hundred kilometres away from Frankfurt Oder, and had hit the motorway with pound signs in his eyes and gone hell for leather in a southerly direction.

Simon cleared the matter up and at the next intersection he turned around and headed back towards Poland and Frankfurt Oder! The journey back was almost four hundred kilometres and by the time we got back to the hotel, we had a cab fare for nearly £320 between us and went straight to work as it was almost 7.30 in the morning. The cab driver must have had a month or two off work with the proceeds of our drunken taxi ride.

I was beginning to wonder to myself where all these little, and sometimes huge problems that kept happening to Scott and I, were of our own doing or somehow or someway self inflicted to a degree. But Germany and being in Germany, seemed the reason behind all of these crazy things that went on and no matter how hard you tried to keep things on a level, if something was going to go wrong, it was going to go wrong for Scott and I big time, no matter how hard we tried.

Since we had been in Germany, and as the recession at home had progressively deepened, more and more Brits had headed into Germany to basically do exactly what Scott and I were doing, which was to survive the recession by doing whatever it took to achieve it. If it meant working sixty hours a week in often terrible working conditions, with little or no attention paid to health and safety, or having to live in substandard accommodation with no water or sanitation, people were doing it, and most people were having to put up with these awful conditions regardless of how bad they were just to pay their mortgages and keep their families fed and watered.

Scott and I thought ourselves quite lucky to have a nice place to live and also we had been paid every week punctually, and received every penny we had earned with no problems as all. This was a huge bonus because talking to other lads, some of them hadn't been paid for four to five weeks and couldn't pay for their digs, and had been thrown out and were sleeping in their cars, hoping to get their money the following day or week. It was not nice seeing people having such huge problems and not having enough money to eat and phone home.

The horror stories were becoming more regular and Scott and I found ourselves doing what we could, whether it was buying a meal or lending some money to them, knowing full well we would not see it again. But little did we know that Frankfurt Oder was about to become our first job where we didn't get paid. It was now Wednesday and Paul had not been up to see us with our last week's wages. None of us were that concerned because where we were working was more than seventy miles from Paul's place, plus he had paid all of us with no problems for over seven months now. Even so, Simon went to a pay phone and called Paul to see exactly what was going on. When he returned he

said, "The Company won't pay Paul until the whole house is finished."
"What do you mean?" I said. "We have to finish all the block work
before they will pay Paul," said Simon. "Yeah, but we work for Paul,
not the Germans, so it's his responsibility to pay us, not them," I said.
"True," said Simon, "But don't worry, we had the same thing last year
and had to wait nearly six weeks to get paid!" "Hang on," said Scott,
"I'm not having this. Paul's a business man, we work for him, and he
pays us regardless of what he's arranged with the Krauts. It's him that
should be taking any risks with his money and not expect us to take
any risks at all. After all, it's him that's making the profit; we're just the
labour force."

Scott was getting very agitated and the more we discussed it, the
worse we all became, until in the end Scott and I went to the phone
box and called Paul ourselves. "What's going on?" I asked Paul as he
picked up the phone. "Has Simon not explained it to you?" said Paul.
"Yes," I replied, "But I'm not having it, we work for you mate not the
bloody Krauts. Get up here and pay us our wages now." "I haven't got
any money to pay you boys at the moment, and until I get a cheque
for the job you're on, I can't pay you." "Bollocks," I said, "You've got
four jobs on the go, and a workforce of over twenty blokes. Don't tell
me you're not making money or are you in business just for the crack.
We're not taking risks with our income, you either sort it out now, or
we'll sort you out," shouted Scott down the phone. "No need to be like

that," said Paul, "You will get your money as soon as the block work's finished," he added, "That's the best I can do." "Not good enough," I replied and hung up.

We walked back to the site, very pissed off and spoke with Simon and Ray about what Paul had said. Simon said, "Don't worry about it; the money will be there as soon as we finish the work. If we walk away, Paul will replace us with four more brickies and our last two week's money will go straight in his pocket. So the best thing to do is finish the next floor and then kick off about it."

It seemed logical, and Scott and I decided to hang it out till the property was completely finished, and after all, it would only take another four or five days to do it. We all had the hump now and threw ourselves into the job. We didn't stop for breakfast or dinner, and just worked until it was too dark to continue. Three days later, we finished the bloody house, and all four of us crammed into the tipper and made our way back to Berlin. Paul's flat was the first port of call and none of us were too happy to see him when he opened the door. "Right, it's finished," said Simon, "And we want part payment now as none of us have a penny to our names." Paul just tutted, which was a silly thing to do under the circumstances and I just about managed to grab Scott's arm as it came flying past my hear, heading in the direction of Paul's nose. Paul owed us the best part of 5 000DM each, and five minutes later we walked away from Paul's flat with the poultry sum of 500DM each, which was better than nothing, I suppose.

We dropped Simon and Ray off outside the Irish pub and made our way back through the rush hour traffic to our little flat. On the way we made the decision to look for another job and another employer in the morning, regardless of what Paul said. We got back to the flat an hour later, the traffic was bumper to bumper all the way, which just made a perfect end to a perfect day, and unbeknown to me, it was just about to become even worse!

As I opened the door, there was a letter on the floor. I picked it up and recognised the handwriting immediately. It was Louise's handwriting. I ripped open the letter; it was very short and to the point. I read something like this:

Dear David,

I've met a man at work who I've been working with for the last 4 and a half months and today I've made up my mind to move in with him.

Regards,

Louise.

No sorry, no apology, no thank you, no warning. I was gutted, I showed Scott the letter. He just stood there with his mouth open in shock. "Come on," he said, "Let's go to Kalle's and have a beer or two." "Ok," I said, "But first I'm going to the phone box to speak to Louise." I called Scott's number and got Jackie. "Is Louise there?" I asked her. "I'm so sorry David," she said, "She moved out last week." "Have you got a phone number or an address for her?" I asked. "No," she replied. "Oh," I said. "If there's anything I can do for you," said Jackie, "Just ask me." "Thank you," I said. "Are you going to be alright?" she asked. "I'll have to be, won't I," I said and added that Scott would be up to call her later, and hung up.

I walked back to Kalle's feeling very low and dejected. Scott passed me on the way and said he was just going to phone Jackie and would be back in about 10 minutes. I was now by this time, as far as I was concerned, almost professional at being single in my life. It still didn't make me feel any better knowing that but even so, I thought I would follow the same course of action that seemed to have helped me in the past, and got absolutely bollocked on lager.

The next day, and surprisingly feeling quite normal, I got up and Scott and I headed for the payphone in order to find ourselves a new job as soon as possible. Scott did all the talking as I was still feeling a little bit pissed and apparently, according to Scott, still slurring my words a little bit as well. "We've got a new job," Scott announced, as he hung up the phone, "And guess where it is," he said. "I'm not in the mood for guessing games," I said. "Spandau," he said with a grin on his face. "Let's go have a looky then," I said. Spandau was a well known area for us and just twenty minutes after leaving the boat yard, we pulled into the address that Scott had written down on an old fag packet.

"We're looking for a guy called Pat," said Scott to one of the biggest black blokes I'd ever seen in all my life. He was absolutely huge, about 6 foot 18 and I would estimate over twenty stone at least with no visible fat on him at all, a giant of a man. He pointed to a cabin and said in an American accent, "He's in that cabin over there." We walked towards the cabin and as we did so, another black bloke walked out from inside. He had to stoop to get under the door frame and when he straightened up, he was even bigger that the guy we had just seen. "Jesus Christ," said Scott, as he walked past us, "Look at the size of him, he must be over 7 feet tall." The bloke stopped and turned around to face us. "Shit," mumbled Scott, under his breath. He walked back towards us and said, "7 feet 2 and a quarter inches actually," and then said "Hi, my name's Keith," and put out a hand towards me. "Hi," I said, "David, nice to meet you." He then shook Scott's hand and wandered off.

"I thought he was going to kick off," said Scott, as he watched Keith walking away. "So did I, and if he had, I think I know who would have come out on top," I said. "Definitely," said Scott. We walked into the cabin and found Pat sat at a desk. "Hi," said Scott, "I called you about the job about an hour ago." Pat, as you might have gathered, was an Irish man. He stood up and in a very, very broad Northern Ireland accent, began talking. Neither Scott nor I caught anything of the first sentence and only a couple of words from the second. Pat began laughing and slowed down to a pace we could both understand. You boys can start tomorrow if you like. "The twins," and he motioned towards the two black lads outside, who were by now loading blocks and bricks out on the over site, "will be here to labour for you, and I'll be here every day to deal with any problems you may have." We thanked Pat and told him we would see him bright and early the next morning.

We met Keith and Kevin, his twin brother, the following morning at 6.45 outside the job waiting to get in. Kevin introduced himself to the both of us and shook hands. His hands were massive, almost twice the size of mine and I've got big hands! "You're American?" said Scott to Keith. "Sure am," said Keith, "We were stationed here in the army and we use to work more often as not at check point Charlie." "We married German girls and when the wall came down, they gave us the option to stay here in Germany, so we did and now we're working for Pat and earning better money," chipped in Kevin.

Pat arrived ten minutes later and twenty minutes later the mortar arrived in a cement lorry. It was the same, warm mortar that Scott and I had used in Holland during the last cold spell. The driver poured it into plastic bins and then placed an insulated blanket over each bin to keep the heat in. Although the weather was still very, very cold, the site was fairly well protected from the wind by the neighbour's fences and hedges, so it felt less exposed and a lot warmer than you would have imagined. Scott and I were enjoying the job and Keith and Kevin were brilliant. They never stopped all day and the house was beginning to take shape very quickly indeed. Pat remained in his office all day, every day, with his gas heater and a fridge full of Guinness and a box of huge cigars, which he chain smoked all day long. By the second week in February, we had all the internal block work up to first floor level, and as Pat didn't want to start the face work until the weather got better, we found ourselves with a few days off while the chippies dealt with concreting the floor.

Three days later, we were back on site going flat out again. Pat paid us, which was the first money Scott and I had received for nearly a month and that nearly completely disappeared paying the rent and heating bills, but at least we had money coming in again. Jackie and the tribe arrived the following Friday night and Scott went to the airport in a taxi to collect them, and we spend the whole evening at Kalle's having a great time. Jackie loved the flat and on the Sunday, we walked across the lake on the ice with the kids, prams and toys to keep the kids amused, to the Papillion pub for dinner and a few beers.

We arrived on site Monday morning; Keith and Kevin as usual, were waiting outside. By 7.30 Pat had still not arrived, so we took the gate off its hinges and carried on as usual. Just after breakfast time, Scott and I were building part of the stairwell, we heard what sounded like a dog yelp. We looked up and saw Keith running across the site with four policemen chasing him. Going in the completely opposite direction was Kevin, also being pursued by four or five policemen. "What the hell is going on?" I said. "Christ knows," said Scott.

Scott and I walked over to the side of the building to get a better view of the proceedings, but as we got to the edge of the slab, we found three police officers standing there pointing pistols at us, and shouting something quite menacingly at us in German. "Oh shit," said Scott, and we just stood there frozen to the spot. The next minute, the whole place was full of police, they handcuffed Scott and I, and manhandled us into separate green and white police vans. I noticed they were the new shape VW campers and thought that might cheer Scott up!

I was handcuffed to a metal rail inside the camper. In front of me was a fold down table and behind it sat this blonde woman in a police uniform? She began banging on in German at me for what seemed like hours, and suddenly stopped, looking at me quizzically. "Sorry love, don't know what you're on about," I said. She threw her hands in the air and jumped out the camper, leaving me chained to the rail, and walked to the next van with Scott inside, who was also chained to the rail. The process was repeated with Scott and obviously with the same result because as she jumped out the van, she was looking very cross indeed.

In the mean time, Keith and Kevin were also in separate police vans, getting much the same treatment as we had received. Ten minutes later, the police vans started up and off we went down the road, the four VWs in front and half a dozen police cars following behind them. As we parked in Spandau police station, my cuffs were removed from the rail and onto the wrist of a copper who resembled Herman Munster. He frog marched me into the police station between two more policemen. Do not pass go, do not collect £200, go straight to jail, and we did. Each of us got thrown into a cell with four policemen and the door was slammed shut behind us.

They removed my hand cuffs and an officer in very bad English, told me to undress. "Piss off," I said, "You didn't even say please." "Take off your clothes," he said again, I thought I had better do as he said, and slowly began to remove my clothes. "Everything," he said, as I stood there in my underpants, so now I was completely naked. The handcuffs went back on and then I was handcuffed to a rail fixed to the wall. They sifted through my clothes, then picked them all up and walked out of the cell, leaving me naked and handcuffed to the wall, and slammed the door behind them.

There was a wooden bench which ran the length of the cell and I could just about sit on it with my arms nearly being pulled out of there sockets because the rail was so high. I sat for a few minutes wondering why the hell we had been banged up, and after a while, began counting the ceramic tiles on the wall and floor. I had just got to 816 when the door flew open and the four gorillas walked back in. They threw my clothes at me and Mr. Bad English told me to get dressed again. As I got dressed, I noticed they had taken my wallet, the keys to the van and the flat. I also had no shoelaces or no belt on my trousers, no cigarettes or lighter, or the gold chain that Louise had bought me for my birthday.

I was now getting over the shock of being arrested and beginning to get rather annoyed. Mr. Bad English then introduced me to his best mate, Mr. Bad Breath, and I was handcuffed on both wrists between the pair of them. We left the cell and walked up to the lift. "Where we going, you little prick?" I said to Mr. Bad English. He looked at me and said, "You bad man, shut up!" "I'll tell you what mate, if you don't loosen these cuffs right now, I'll show you what a bad man can do," I said. He just looked at me in disgust.

We exited the lift, and walked into a brightly lit room with a big mirror on one wall, obviously an identification room. The lights were shinning straight into my eyes and as we walked in, five other men, approximately the same age and build as me, walked in behind us. I noticed they also all had long blonde hair like mine. Mr. Bad English and Mr. Bad Breath undid my cuffs and told me to stand still and face the mirror. The lights dimmed momentarily and then came back on even brighter than they had been before. I stood for what seemed hours but was probably only ten minutes. The lights dimmed again and in came my two new mates again.

Once cuffed again, we were off this time still on the same floor. "I want a phone call now you Pratt," I said to Mr. Bad English. He just looked at me and carried on walking. I stopped dead which took the pair of them by surprise. "Get me a fucking translator and a bloody telephone," I said. By now I was about to completely loose my temper and I meant it, but was not really in a position to make demands.

Mr. Bad Breath pulled his gun out of his holster and as Mr. Bad English couldn't because he was handcuffed to me on the left hand side and couldn't reach it. I looked at Mr. Bad Breath; he was pointing a gun at me. "Translator and a telephone," I said again. He just waved the pistol in the direction of the door at the end of the hallway and began to walk off. I stood my ground and looking back on this moment, it was probably not a good idea, but in for a penny and all that, I screamed at him, "Get me a fucking translator and a telephone now!" Two seconds later the hallway was full of police and I was physically dragged through the double doors and bundled into cell.

I think about an hour passed. I was just guessing as I didn't have my watch. The door opened and in came my new best mates again, but this time they had two more friends with them. We followed the same procedure as before, cuffed on both sides and now off we went again, one on each side and now one in front of me and one behind me. We walked up the corridor into another room just up from the cell. They sat me at a metal desk in the middle of the room and cuffed me to it. Ten minutes elapsed and in walked two women in lab coats and began setting up various bits and pieces on the table. I had my finger prints taken, my palm prints take; they also made a plaster cast of each of my trainer soles and then they took a swab from my mouth.

In walked two suits with ties on and sat on the two chairs in front of me. They handed me three pieces of A4 paper, all neatly typed in German. I looked at it, obviously I couldn't read it and I handed it back to them. It was then again offered to me, but this time with a ball point pen. The uglier of the two suits began to speak to me in very, very good English and said if you sign this statement, you can go home. "Listen mate," I said, "For one, I don't read German so you can forget that, plus I don't know what the hell is going on, and until I get legal representation and a translator, you can poke that lot up your arse." He understood that alright, and two minutes later, I was back in my cell again.

Unbeknown to any of us at the time, Pat had seen us being driven away and had, by knowing the right people, managed to get hold of someone from the British embassy, who was on their way and was apparently going to sort out the whole mess. Nonetheless, we were in the cells now and would remain there until our saviour turned up.

The following morning breakfast arrived, and was an insipid puddle of yuck that smelt quite strange so I chose not to eat it, but drank down just the coffee as I was so thirsty. An hour after that I found myself being cuffed again between the two idiots and marched off to the lifts again. As we approached I saw Scott already standing by the lifts. He heard us coming and turned his head in my direction. As I got closer, I could see he had two black eyes and a split lip! "What happened to you?' I asked as we all stood waiting for the lifts to arrive. "I was cuffed to the wall and one of the Muppets set about me with a truncheon," he said. "Bloody hell, are you ok?" I asked. "Think so," he said, "But I think I've got a busted rib," he added.

The lift arrived and we all crammed into it. "Ladies underwear please, third floor," I said as the doors closed. Scott laughed and then winced as his lip began to bleed. "How come you've got two coppers?" he asked, as he only had one. "They told me I'm a bad man," I said and we both laughed this time.

Standing in the foyer was Pat, along side him was a big tall man in a suit. Pat smiled as we walked up. "You boys alright?" he asked. "Not really," I replied, "They've had a pop at Scott, which may need medical attention." "Bloody hell," said Pat, looking at Scott's face. Mr. Bad English and Mr. Bad Breath released me from the cuffs and went to walk away. I tapped Mr. Bad English on the shoulder, as he turned towards me I said to him, "If I see you in the street mate, I will kill you,

you wanker." He just shrugged his shoulders and walked away. "That scared him," said Scott, and we both began to laugh again.

Keith and Kevin turned up and now we all stood by the front desk. Pat introduced us to Mr. James and he explained what had happened. Next to the building site was a home for old age pensioners and also for the mentally instable. There had been an aggravated assault and robbery at the home some three days previously. One of the loonies had walked past our site, seen us all working there and reported to the police that we were the people responsible for the crime. "Brilliant," said Scott, "So now what happens?" Mr. James stepped into the chair, "Well what happens now is you can all go home as the police have caught the perpetrators last night and you're free to go." "Well, I want a complaint form," said Scott, "Look at my face." "So do I," said Keith, opening his mouth, he had lost his two front teeth. "And I want an apology and compensation," I said. "I'll do my best," said Mr. James. "Make sure you do," said Kevin, with quite a lot of venom is his voice. The desk sergeant then began getting our personal belongings out and dumped them on the desk in front of him.

I picked up my watch and my wallet, which was now completely empty! "So what do you think about that then Mr. James?" I said. "We'll file a complaint form before we leave," he said. "Mine's empty too," said Scott, rather indignantly. "And mine," said Keith. "Let me deal with this," said Mr. James, "I'll get back to you later with the results, its best you get off home now." Pat took us back to the site and bless him; he gave us all 400DM each to keep us going. We jumped in the tipper and headed for home.

Jackie, was to say, the least happy to see us back home and had been absolutely frantic with worry, as she had no one to phone to see what had happened to us, but was relieved to see us alright. She couldn't believe what we had just been through.

By the end of February, the weather was slowly, very slowly beginning to warm up a little and by the time Jackie went home, the ice was beginning to melt on the lake. The police were patrolling the area now, stopping people walking on it, in fear of people falling through it and drowning.

Jackie and Scott had had a long talk during the week and between them, they had decided that it would be better for Jackie and the kids to come and live in Germany, and rent their house out until such time as we could go back home and earn a decent income in England. At least Scott would see the kids and the recession at home did not look as if it was about to end in any way, shape or form.

Three weeks later, we had the flat completely full with Jackie and the tribe, and just five days later; I began to understand what Louise had kept going on about. The noise was absolutely terrible, the baby was screaming continuously and the rest of the kids were making so much noise and mess it was totally unbelievable. I began staying out a bit later at night, hoping by the time I got home the kids would be in bed and it would be a bit quieter. But no such luck was to be had. The noise remained at a constant level, bloody loud; it was making me grumpy as it was disrupting my sleep pattern. I had to do something about it, either that or spend all my time constantly tired. Plus the fact that the flat was not really big enough for all of us and Jackie was also due to pop another one out in less than two months time.

Pat's job finished a couple of weeks later and he asked us if we would be interested in starting another one for him. We readily agreed and found ourselves a few days later on a huge development the size of which we had never seen before. It was massive and as luck would have it, still just the other side of Spandau and less than half an hour's drive from the boat yard. The site was multiracial and multicultural; there were hundreds of people working there from all over Europe, Poles, Italians, English, German, also a few Russian and Eastern block gangs who were mostly working as labourers.

The total amount of English I would estimate was over a hundred and fifty at least, and they were all working for various different subcontractors, from German to English, just as Scott and I were. Pat's team consisted of nearly twenty five bricklayers and five or six labourers; we got our tools out, found a spot and jumped in. Scott and I had not been working more than five minutes when all of a sudden the site was swarming with police again. "Not again," said Scott. "I hope not," I replied.

We saw various people running off in all directions being chased by police. Pat walked up and said, "Don't worry, they're only looking for illegal immigrants and people without relevant paper work to work here in Germany." Scott and I breathed a sigh of relief and carried on working.

Every Thursday, Pat would arrive and walk around the site with a rather nice looking German girl who was responsible for measuring the work we had done, in order to pay Pat. I began to look forward to Thursdays and ogling this nice looking girl, wandering around with a tape and a clipboard. Scott had noticed my interest in the girl and basically began taking the Mickey. "Go and have a chat with her," he would say, trying to push me into her path as she walked around. "Yeah, she's probably married anyway," I said. "It wouldn't hurt to ask now would it?" he said. "Suppose not," I said, "But what if she can't speak English?" "Pat speaks German, ask him," said Scott. "Nah can't be bothered," I said. Scott sloped off and before I knew it, had returned with Pat and the girl! "You sly bugger," I said to Scott, "What the hell have you said?" I asked him. "I told him you fancy the pants off her," said Scott. "Oh god," I said, "Thanks a bunch." Pat was grinning and said something to the girl in German. She then walked up to me, shook my hand and said, "Hello David, my name is Ushi, how nice to meet you." I just stood there like and idiot. "Say something then," said

Scott, "You Muppet." "Err, err, oh, um yeah, err…" I said.

Pat stepped in and rattled off something in German. He then turned to me and said, "You're going out with her on Friday night at eight O'clock; meet her at the Irish pub for a drink at 7.30." "Ok," I said. Ushi turned and smiled and promptly walked off with Pat and her clipboard, leaving me with a stunned look on my face. "Easy as falling off a log," said Scott, grinning at me. "You sod," I said, "That really embarrassed me, I'm capable of doing my own chatting up mate. Thanks." "Well, it worked didn't it," said Scott. "I'll let you know Friday!" I replied.

As the recession deepened at home, I noticed that the age group of people coming to work in Germany started to creep up too. It was no longer just the twenty-something's and thirty-something's that were doing it. All of a sudden it was the forty and fifty-something's descending into Germany in droves; every week you began to see new faces and new cars in the car parks on site or in the pubs. The funny thing was, well I found it quite amusing anyway, was most of this particular age group were normally married and had been married for a considerable amount of their lives, but when they arrived in Germany on their own or with mates from the building industry, they all of a sudden became complete party animals. From being 2.2 kids, half a Labrador, wash the car on Sunday, pub on Friday and sex on their birthday (if lucky), they turned into the beer monsters from hell causing more problems than the average bunch of eighteen year olds; I'd never seen anything like it.

Last orders at home were at 10.30 plus twenty minutes drinking up time. In Germany the pubs closed when they chose to close, which meant should you want to, you could basically sit in a pub all night long and drink until the doctors came to take you away! Some, no, most of this age group, seemed to be hell bent on proving a point, that being they could drink like a fish every night of the week and have almost a second go at being single again. Loonies! I would watch these guys, over the weeks, slowly but surely sinking further and further into a routine; work, pub, work, pub, work, pub, and then you would see them drinking at work as well. If only their wives could see them, they would have been hung, drawn and quartered.

I had always thought to myself the eighteen to twenty five year olds were the landlord's nightmare, but having seen this age group perform, I now had to change my mind! I have always enjoyed people watching but this was something else. It was almost a competition or it seemed to be who could drink the most, who could start the most fights, who could get arrested the most, who could brag the most; the list was never ending. It was a great source of amusement for me and for them it was almost a second childhood.

Anyway, I'm rambling again, back to the story! Friday arrived and I thought I had better make an effort to look presentable, I even ironed my shirt, well Jackie did anyway, and I asked Scott to drop me at the bus stop as it was raining quite hard, well hard enough to make me look like a drowned rat if I had walked to the bus stop.

I arrived at the Irish pub at seven and found myself a seat at the bar and began to thumb my way through my pocket German-English dictionary with a view of constructing a sentence in German, as my opening gambit, and hopefully something that might make her smile or even laugh.

I needn't have worried; Ushi turned up bang on 7.30 and was armed with an electronic keypad type pocket translator. It was a great piece of kit and even with all the noise in the pub, we were still managing to communicate albeit it was taking a long time but we were getting there slowly. By nine O'clock I had learned more German with the help of this little machine than I had managed to pick up in the last eight months. It was brilliant and on top of that, I now had expert help from a rather lovely blonde German woman, who seemed to be on a mission to get me speaking German. She suggested that we went for something to eat and ten minutes later we walked into Japanese sushi restaurant, the rest of the evening was a bit of a blur, as we managed to polish off a couple of bottles of Saki between us. Eventually with a bit of help from the little translator, I managed to invite her to Kalle's to meet Scott and Jackie and watch the antics of the transvestites Travesty show.

How the hell I got home that night still remains to this a day a complete mystery to me but I awoke the next morning back at the flat, still fully clothed in my bed with Scott leaning over me. "Are you getting up or what?" he said, "It's nearly six and time to go to work you Muppet!"

"Well, how did ya get on?" asked Scott, as we drove to work ten minutes later. "I don't know quite honestly," I replied. "What?!" said Scott. "I got absolutely hammered on Saki," I replied. "You nutter," said Scott, and then added, "Are you seeing her again?" "Yeah, she's coming to Kalle's tonight to watch the transvestite show, and have a bite to eat," I said, "That was the only part of the night's proceedings that I could remember clearly!"

We arrived at work some ten minutes later and found the gates still locked shut. Everyone was milling around outside; there were cars and vans, and also a few Lorries parked everywhere waiting to get into the site. Scott and I wandered around for a bit and by eight O'clock people started getting the hump and began leaving in ones and twos. Half an hour later, we followed suit and made our way back home. We were not going to waste any time standing around doing nothing and earning nothing!

Things happen for a reason. I'm a great believer in that and when we got back to the flat; it only went to prove it yet again to me. Jackie's waters had broken and she was in a terrible state. The kids were screaming and Jackie was crying; it was total mayhem in the flat. I rushed down to Kalle's and asked him if he would be kind enough to phone for an ambulance as Jackie was about to give birth. He very kindly obliged and twenty minutes later they turned up outside and bundled Jackie and Scott inside and flew off with lights and sirens blaring.

Now this was something we had not discussed between ourselves at all, and was completely new to me. I now had four kids; David, Millie, Clare and Chloe to deal with. I knew they needed feeding and entertaining and unfortunately I also knew they would need 'cleaning.' Yuck, I wasn't looking forward to that bit at all and as I had never before had to do it, I was trying as hard as I could not to think about it anyway.

As Jackie had left, she had shown me who ate what and where everything was so at least I had a rough idea as to what to feed them and what size nappies fitted what sized bums. Oh god, what had I let myself in for? I was not going to enjoy this one little bit. I grabbed David, who was still wearing his 'I am 5' t-shirt and together with Millie, who was nearly 4 now, and plonked them both in front of the TV. I rummaged through a pile of videos and found one David had got for his birthday the week before, and slammed it in the video. Right, that's that, I thought, and turned around to find Chloe bouncing up and down in her baby bouncer. As I looked more closely, I saw there was now shit seeping out both sides of her nappy. Oh shit, I thought. Clare was standing next to her pointing and holding her nose. "She's smelly, David," she said to me. "I know, sweetheart," I replied. As I released Chloe from the bouncer, David and Millie began screaming at each other. "I don't want to watch Batman," said Millie. "I do, I do," said David. Bloody hell, I thought, I now had Chloe in my arms stinking the place out and Clare following behind me still holding her nose and pointing to Chloe saying, "Stinky bum, stinky bum," while David and Millie were about to kill each other.

I ejected the Batman tap and managed to find a Captain Pugwash tape and quickly slammed it in the video player, as by now Chloe's nappy was not only leaking out both sides but also down the front of my shirt and trousers. "Oh god, I don't need this," I said out loud. I found Chloe's changing mat and eventually, after a bit of trial and error, managed to clean her up and get a fresh clean nappy on her. I put her back in the baby bouncer and strapped her securely in place. I checked everyone was ok and stripped off and jumped quickly into the shower. I had just got the shampoo into my hair and world war III broke out again. Millie was screaming, so I grabbed my towel and ran into the sitting room. The floor was laminated wood, so as I tried to stop, my feet were still soaking wet, I slid first on my feet and secondly on my arse, straight into the opposite wall. The noise I made hitting the wall stopped the screaming instantly and now all eyes were on me, on the floor. By now the towel was gone and I found myself completely naked on the floor smothered in shampoo. David and Millie were now jumping up and down next to me. "Can we play, can we play David?" they shouted at me in unison.

Scott and Jackie had been gone less than half an hour, but it already felt to me like a fortnight. I got back into the shower and five minutes later, I was sat in front of the TV, watching Captain Pugwash with David and Millie. Clare was standing next to Chloe, bouncing her up and down in her bouncer. Peace had at last been achieved. Thank God!

The last time I had watched Captain Pugwash was as a kid in the 70s, but I was now watching it as an adult. It was brilliant! Rodger the cabin boy and seaman stains? How Barbara Whitehouse had never managed to ban this show I would never know. I sat there with the kids, chuckling away to myself and watched all six episodes with them. Clare announced she wanted a poo-poo and off I went again. The day progressed in much the same vein all day long but the only time it was totally quiet, was when we had dinner which was a simple affair of ham and cheese with crisps and orange squash, and a bottle of milk for Chloe. By five O'clock, I was totally knackered and had begun to wonder how the hell Jackie had managed to do this day in and day out without complaining once. Since this day, I've had nothing but respect for women who can multi-task with kids; cooking, washing and also husbands or boyfriends to boot!

The doorbell rang at just before 6.30 and clutching baby Chloe, I opened the door. There stood Kalle, and next to him was Ushi! She just stood there gawping at me. Kalle beat a hasty retreat and I invited her in. The house looked as if it had just been vacated by squatters! There was crap everywhere; toys, books, bicycles and all sorts of junk scattered everywhere. I dumped Chloe back into her bouncer and made a place for Ushi to sit on the settee, simply by chucking all the rubbish on the floor.

After about half an hour with the electronic translator, I had managed to explain exactly what had happened to Ushi, and at last saw her face begin to soften as she now understood that the kids were not mine but Scott and Jackie's. Phew, that could have been the end of it, I thought!

As luck would have it, Scott walked back in the door not twenty minutes later with a huge grin on his face. "I'm a dad again," he said proudly, and then added, "Just over 3kg, we've decided to call him Ryan." "Nice one, mate," I said and shook his hand. "Right, your turn," I said and grabbed Ushi and headed for the door. "Thanks," said Scott, "For looking after the kids, have a good time and I'll see you later."

Kalle's restaurant was chocker block with people, but we managed to get a table at the front because all the regulars knew that anyone who was stupid enough to want to sit at the front would, without fail, become an instant target for the transvestites and their particular form of audience participation! Nonetheless, it was the last table, so we had no choice as far as I was concerned.

I ordered drinks while looking through the menu. I already knew what I was going to have; it was the same as I always had, predictably steak and chips. Ushi ordered a salad almost big enough to feed a small bird and presently Kalle arrived with the drinks. I'd never met a girl that drank pints, I was well impressed! Kalle decided to be a nosey bastard and plonked himself down at our table and immediately began to give me the third degree about my new acquaintance. Who was she, where had I met her, what did she do? The questions were endless but the biggest mistake he had actually made without realising it himself, was to sit at our table because not two minutes later, in walked the transvestites, all six of them wearing Indian saris with their faces completely covered. They saw Kalle and before he had a chance to escape and hide at a safe distance behind the bar, grabbed him. It was something they had obviously been trying to do for a long time and Kalle was trying his hardest to escape but they had him now and he wasn't going anywhere, if the trannies could help it. The regulars in the restaurant were going crazy; I guess they thought it was also about time that Kalle got his comeuppance.

Each week that I had seen the Travesty Show, they had become more and more complicated. I suppose in an effort to keep the audience amused and also the transvestites in work. This week was no exception, and Kalle had even popped up coloured spot lights for them. The show began; they ripped off their saris and beneath the saris revealed spiked and studded leather underwear, and the compulsory high length leather high heel boots. The crowd went mental clapping and cheering. The trannies were pouting and parading around in front of the bar lapping up the applause and the cheering. Kalle was led off to the back of the restaurant and reappeared two minutes later, minus his shirt and with a spiked dog collar around his neck, being led like a dog on a lead into the centre of the bar stage area.

By now, the whole place was on its feet clapping and cheering. Kalle was led up to a piece of plywood which was leaning against the wall in the corner. I hadn't noticed it as I came in but it had the shape of a human body on it outlined in black paint. On each corner were some Velcro straps and Kalle was fixed arms and legs wide to each corner by the straps. Next, one of the trannies walked up to our table and grabbed Ushi by the hand and dragged her out in front of the bar. He opened a brief case and handed her fourteen enormous great big carving knives! Then he showed her how to hold them by the blade and motioned for her to throw them in the direction of Kalle. Before she had time to react, he pulled a blindfold out of the briefcase and covered her eyes with it. Kalle was by now, nearly having a nervous breakdown and trying his hardest to escape his confinement, but to no avail. Next, the transvestite blindfolded Kalle!

Once this was done, he removed Ushi's blindfold and showed her back to her seat. A drum roll began to sound; Kalle was now screaming and was obviously not a happy bunny at all. The drum roll stopped and the transvestite, who was standing next to Kalle holding a small hammer, hit the plywood right next to Kalle's left ear. Kalle shouted something obviously quite rude, as everyone began to cheer. The drum roll began again and abruptly stopped. The trannie hit the plywood with the hammer next to Kalle's right ear this time. Again he shouted something out. The crowd went wild, and so it went on fourteen times. Kalle was now a nervous wreck and still shouting obscenities from his plywood prison. At last, Kalle's blindfold was removed and the drum roll began again. As it stopped yet again, the trannie banged the plywood with the hammer to show Kalle exactly what had been going on while he had been blindfolded. Kalle began to laugh, as did the whole restaurant. It was a brilliant idea, and Kalle had been nearly crapping himself thinking the noise was actually the knives hitting the wood!

The rest of their show was a bit of an anticlimax, but even so it was still very funny and now Kalle was circulating again, he was being ridiculed by the locals for being such a baby. It was another good night and my new friend had obviously enjoyed herself as well. On parting some hours later, Ushi thrust her phone number into my hand on a napkin and told me to call her. We said a very polite goodnight and both went our separate ways.

Sunday morning, Scott and I drove down to Spandau hospital and I was introduced to baby Ryan for the first time. Jackie looked absolutely knackered; it had been a long labour and had taken it out of her. "How are you feeling, sweetheart?" I asked her. "Tired," she managed to say with a struggle. "Is this the last one in the family?" I asked Scott. "Dunno," he replied and added that they had always spoken of having at least 6 kids! "You're completely off your heads," I said to both of them, "Absolute nutters, completely bonkers!" Jackie was, according to her doctor, to remain in hospital for five days. This also meant that Scott was going to have to stay at the flat and take care of the kids. I didn't envy him one bit at all!

So on Monday morning, I found myself driving to work on my own, while Scott, already at just gone six in the morning, had his hands full of kids demanding food, TV and anything else they could wangle out of him. I arrived at work twenty minutes later. The site gates were still shut up tight. I parked up and eventually found Pat talking to some of the lads. He waved me over and told me that the company had just gone bankrupt. The site was shut until the receivers arrived to sort it all out. "What about our tools and things?" I said. "I'll try and get then for you later today," he replied, "And I will also try and get your money as well as I've not yet got the payment from last week," he added. Brilliant, I thought, looks like we've been done again and pottered of home again to break the bad news to Scott.

On arriving back home, I broke the news to Scott and also then added that we couldn't even go and find another job yet as all our tools were also still locked up at the site! "Bloody typical," he said. The rest of the week we stayed at home, phoning Pat everyday to find out about our tools and also the possibility of getting our money, but each day yielded much the same result. So, each day we phoned again to see if there had been any new developments.

Jackie came back home on the Thursday with baby Ryan and I now knew it was definitely time for me to go looking for somewhere new to live, as five kids and three adults in our tiny flat was probably going to push me over the edge if I stayed any longer. I went down to Kalle's restaurant and found a couple of copies of the local paper and began thumbing through it looking for the flats to rent section. I rung a few that I through may be possibilities and asked Kalle for a coffee. He was quite taken aback by the request for coffee as it was normally a beer that I ordered and he then asked me what the problem was. I explained that the new arrival of Ryan now made the grand total of eight including myself in the flat and it was time I found a place of my own to rent, basically so I could get some peace and quiet, and also be able to sleep at night as the kids made so much noise.

"You can rent the flat over my restaurant if you want," said Kalle. "I didn't know you had a flat here," I replied. "Yes," said Kalle, "I only use it when I've had too much to drink and can't drive home. Come and have a look if you want to." We walked through the restaurant and up a flight of stairs in the corner. At the top of the stairs was a small landing area with a window that looked over the lake. Kalle got a key out of his pocket and opened the door. The flat was lovely, all furnished in a German wood sort of style, but still very nice. It had two bedrooms, one bathroom, a massive kitchen and a very long thin lounge which had a balcony the full length of it outside.

We haggled over the price and eventually came up with a nice round figure of a 1000DM a month, bills not included. Kalle said he would get a contract drawn up, but I could move in any time I wanted to. I thanked him and I really meant it because it was so handy still being close enough to Scott so we could both still use the van to get to work. Scott and Jackie were quite shocked when I told them I was moving out and Jackie got quite upset so I walked her to the kitchen window. "I'm only going there," I said pointing at my new balcony; it was no more than 30m away. "That's ok then," she said, cheering up a bit.

I suddenly remembered that I hadn't phoned Ushi, and began searching for the napkin she had given me, with her number on it. Nearly two hours later, after turning the house upside down and the van, I found it in my pocket and wandered up to the pay phone to call her. Now, my German was still much the same as it had been before. I could ask for a beer, I could ask where the toilets were, I could say please and thank you. As I dialled her number, I began to think it's going to be a very short and quite strange conversation, if all I can say to her is hello, can I have a beer, where are the toilets, and thank you. She's going to think I'm a complete nutter, or at least a little strange. I decided to opt out of the German mode and instead went for the English approach and just spoke in English to her when she answered the phone. I said, "Do you fancy meeting up for a drink or eats at Kalle's tonight?" "Ja," she replied. "Ok, that's great," I said and hung up, just in case she started rambling on at me in German and got me completely and totally confused.

I wandered back to Kalle's with a view, as it was yet again Saturday night, of finding a table out of the firing line of the trannies and managed to get a table far enough away as to be no threat at all; at least I hoped so! Twenty minutes later in walked Ushi and my god, she was almost wearing a mini skirt. I couldn't keep my eyes off her, she looked absolutely great. As she walked in, everyone was watching her. She walked up to me smiling and thrust a box into my hand and gave me a quick peck on the cheek. "What's all this?" I asked her. She motioned to me to open it, so I ripped it open. Inside was a German language course on cassettes and a Sony walkman. "Bloody hell," I said, and added, "Thank you very much; it's very kind of you!"

We spent the rest of the evening talking with the help of her electronic translator and were so engrossed we never even noticed the Travesty act in progress, and by the end of the evening, I had persuaded her to meet with me during the week for another chat and a drink or two. On Monday with the help of Pat, Scott and I managed to retrieve our tools from the site, but unfortunately Pad had as yet not managed to get any of our money for us, but offered us another job should we want it. Of course we wanted it, we were bloody skint!

This was our first job in what used to be East Germany, and was in a very small town called Hoppergarten. Pat explained to us and a few other trades, what needed to be done on the job as we walked around. The job itself was on the old horse racing track. It was very, very dilapidated and needed completely renovating to bring it back up to the standard for international horse racing, and Pat had got the job to do it from a West Germany company who had bought the race track; lock, stock and barrel.

Pat had secured the whole job for himself, and was supplying all materials and labour. The work force was all English and Irish, which meant there would be no language problems to contend with either, which was great for us. In total, there were more than sixty tradesmen on the job; from ground workers, plumbers, chippies, brickies, sparky's and also a few painters and decorators. The site was run just like an English site, which suited Scott and me fine, and we were now working in a small gang of six brickies and two labourers. As Pat had given us basically a free reign to start where we wanted, and follow round behind the ground workers, it was working like clock work and almost like working back home in England.

The weather started to warm up quite quickly and by mid-April, it was getting quite warm, warm enough to sit outside in the beer garden at Kalle's in the evenings for the odd beer or two. At work it would have been the start of the flat racing season on the race track, but as it was being totally renovated there would be no racing until the spring of 1991.

The hotel, restaurant and bar that looked over the race track was now losing a lot of trade, so they bought in a load of TVs, got a few satellite dishes and began to televise greyhound racing and horse racing mostly as it happens from the English dog tracks and Dutch horse racing tracks. The English and Irish lads, once they had found out about the new 'betting shop', seemed to spend most of their spare time and probably most of their money, sat in front of the TV screens, screaming at the dogs and horses to win. That was apart from two chippies, who had over the days and weeks, made an awful lot of money from it. Scott and I had never been into gambling but in the end, our curiosity got the better of us and we wandered over for a chat with the two lads.

It turned out that Colin and Paul's father had a betting shop in Hull and with the help of this insider information from their dad, they were managing to win an average of 6 out of every ten races by phoning him quickly before the start of every race. A few weeks later, both Colin and Paul gave up full time work with Pat and sat every day in the betting shop making loads of money between them. Thank you. The rest of Pat's mob got wind of what they were doing and a few of the lads, maybe six or eight, tried to do the same by following the bets that Colin and Paul were putting on. It worked for all of them for a little while, until they started to get over greedy. Instead of placing small bets, the stakes they were putting down became higher and higher. Colin and Paul suggested to the lads to keeps the bets at a reasonable level, or the betting shop would not be able to cover the bets. Did they listen? No they did not, not at all.

As Scott and I sat in the betting shop waiting on a Friday night for Pat to arrive with our pay. The row between Colin and Paul and the other lads was beginning to escalate, as yet again the bets were becoming too large. The local Germans were also getting rather annoyed with the fact that the English kept on winning such large amounts of money and were also chipping in with the odd insult or dirty look. I could hear Colin next to me saying, "Look, just put £10 on it to win, not £50. You will end up ruining it for us all, or I and Paul will move on to another betting shop!" The answer was as I predicted to Scott; "Piss off Colin, mind your own fucking business, we'll do what we want." Suddenly a cheer went up; another dog had come in at seven-one. I turned up and watched the woman from the betting shop count out the equivalent of about £80 into Colin's hand. The next thing I knew was hitting the bar. Some idiot had hit me across the back of the head with a bar stool!

Looking back on it now, I know the chair was meant for Colin, but unfortunately the guy was a lousy shot and got me instead.

I sat there stunned, looking at the bar top; my two caps I had done in Holland after the camper crash, and now also another one lay beside them. I had also nearly bitten through my tongue, there was claret everywhere. I couldn't see Scott but I felt him literally jump over my back as I sat there still looking at my teeth on the bar! That was it, it all kicked off. People everywhere knocking the living shit out of each other; about twelve English lads and about twenty Germans all going for it big time. It lasted all of maybe four or five minutes and then in rushed the local old bill with truncheons, and started battering everyone and anyone in sight, me included.

We were all cuffed and yes you guessed it, dragged off down to Spandau police station yet again! This time was a lot quicker than the last and within an hour, we had all been booked and released and summoned to appear in court the following Friday. We went straight to Spandau hospital and I found myself an emergency dentist who, although he was a bit of a butcher, managed to make me yet again another set of temporary teeth. It's always been my bloody teeth, always! I eventually walked back out to find Scott and when he saw me, he just began laughing. "What's up with you?" I asked. "It's those teeth," said Scott, "They make you look like the vicar out of the dick every show." "Thanks a bunch," I said. But he was right, they were huge and also a strange off-white colour, but they would have to do regardless of how they looked.

The following Friday rolled around far too quickly for my liking, and we found ourselves standing in court along with twenty seven other lads all looking much the same as us. Worried would describe it to a tee! We stood there watching the three judges walking in. They all sat simultaneously, looked down at the paperwork in front of them and studied it for approximately five minutes. Then one of them looked up and began talking very, very quickly in German and all the time looking at us all over the top of his old fashioned glasses. I managed to get maybe two or three words from the whole onslaught, which lasted for about ten minutes. At last we walked out of the court and Pat immediately joined us in the foyer of the courthouse to inform us as to what the judge had said.

Pat said we had all been fined 500DM each, plus court fees and had been banned from using the betting shop for a period of three months. Not too bad really I thought, considering the damage that had been done during the fight. The only downside was now we would not be able to get food or anything to drink during the day at work from the restaurant and as it was the only place in Hoppergarten to actually buy anything to eat, we would now have to bring food and drink with us each day.

April was gone and in came May with a vengeance. The temperature was rising daily and was it rising like mad! My god it was hot, bloody hot. It seemed years ago that it was minus something horrible and icy, and now we were working in a furnace. The air was still which made you sweat; there was no rest bite from the sun's ever increasing temperature. We began starting work an hour early in the mornings at six O'clock to try and beat the heat of the midday and afternoon sun.

After work in the evenings, we spent on the beach by the boat yard. It was great; barbeques on the beach and swimming in the lake, the water temperature was fairly warm and the evenings were still light until 9.30 or ten O'clock.

Ushi and I were now seeing each other almost everyday and I was enjoying her company. My German was by now getting better by the day and with the language course and the translator, I was actually able to have a conversation with her totally in German. I was very impressed with myself but then armed with my new found language skills, I did the unthinkable, and yet again opened my mouth without engaging the thing in my skull, you know, the brain thing, and asked her if she would like to move in with me! The next four evenings after work were spent transporting, firstly her shoe and handbag collection and then the rest of her belongings into the flat, from her brother's house where she had been living in Spandau. At last everything was done, and we went to Kalle's to celebrate along with Scott, Jackie and the tribe.

During the meal, Scott said that he wanted to go back to England to pick the camper up as it was impossible to transport his ever increasing family around without using taxis everywhere. So we decided to drive back home with the tipper and sell it in England and split the proceeds of the sale between us.

Monday morning, we explained to Pat our intentions regarding going home for a few days and that evening, Scott and I headed off towards Hamburg and the ferry. Unusually, customs were, I think, totally asleep or on a tea break or something because for the first time in a very, very long time, both Scott and I sailed through customs without so much as a, 'would you come this way please sir' or a single remark about the way we looked. We were absolutely; completely gob smacked, and hoped it would be as simple upon our return with the camper.

The ferry was only about a quarter full and the journey home was, to be quite honest, a little boring because of the lack of passengers. There was no people-watching to be done and almost all of the bars and restaurants were closed, so Scott and I elected to have an early night and slept the boring trip away.

Norwich was also trauma free and we came straight off the ferry and drove through passport control and customs without a problem. "Most unusual," I said to Scott as we headed for home. He agreed but then added, "It wouldn't last." I knew he was probably right. We drove straight to the White Horse, parked up and went in. Mary was working behind the bar and almost passed out when she saw Scott and I walk in. We hadn't thought to phone home to let anyone know we were arriving but nonetheless, we received a hero's welcome along with something to eat and lashings of Stella.

The following morning, nursing the first hangover that we had had for months, we trundled off in the tipper, firstly back to the garage we had bought it from to find out the balance we owed on it and after a bit of haggling, sold the tipper back to them. But after we had paid off the balance we owed, we ended up with just over £1000 which was a bit depressing. But the redeeming thing was it was cash, cash, cash. When we eventually got back to the White Horse after about fourteen busses, one train and a taxi, we found Malcolm and Mary waiting for us out the front of the pub. "This looks serious," I said to Scott." "Yeah, it does," he replied.

"What's up dad?" asked Scott to Malcolm. "It's your camper," Malcolm said. Scott immediately went into meltdown mode even before Malcolm had time to finish what he was saying. The air was blue and Scott was on a roll! As hard as he could try, Malcolm could not get a word in edgeways and eventually bellowed, "Shut up!" to Scott so loudly it had made me jump out of my skin. Malcolm gave Scott the keys to the garage and Scott stomped off towards the back of the pub to inspect what he had assumed was damage to his beloved VW camper van. I heard the VW start up and two minutes later, Scott drove around the front of the pub with a stupid grin on his face. He jumped out and hugged his mum and dad. "Thanks guys," he said. "Well," I said to Scott, "Would you like to tell me what's going on please?" "Look at this," he said to me as he walked around the side of the camper. "What am I looking at?" I asked him. "Just look," he said again. "Still can't see what I'm looking at," I replied. "I'll tell you," said Malcolm suddenly. "Ok, please do," I said, "Put me out of my misery?" "We've put awning rails on both sides and bought two new awnings, one for each side," said Malcolm. Scott was ecstatic with it, I hadn't seen him smile so much in ages. It was a nice gesture from Mary and Malcolm as well. "I suppose this is your way of saying, can you and mum come and visit us in Germany," said Scott to Malcolm. "At lease we'll have somewhere to sleep now," said Mary, laughing.

It was time to get moving, we had a ferry to catch. We said our goodbyes to Malcolm and Mary and jumped into the camper. As we pulled off, I mentioned to Scott that I needed to pop into my parents' house just to show my mum and dad I was still alive and kicking, and had not been abducted by aliens or anything equally as horrible. We pulled into my parents' driveway and walked straight in as the front door was already open. There in the living room were my parents, and also my grandparents who I hadn't seen for quite a while. In fact, I think it must have been over a year or more at least.

Unlike Mary and Malcolm, who had almost died of shock when

we walked into the White Horse, the reaction we received was a lot more subdued at my house. To be quite honest, I wasn't at all surprised in the least when we were almost totally ignored by both my mum and dad, who were in deep conversation with my grandparents. My father eventually grunted a hello and my mother asked if we were hungry. Both Scott and I declined and headed for the fridge in the hope of finding something maybe alcoholic to drink in an attempt to survive the situation, or at least to dull it a tad. My grandad was not a talkative man at all but without warning he just began talking to me. "I hear you're now living and working in Germany," he said, and before I could answer, Scott jumped in and said, "He's also got a German girlfriend as well." Thanks Scott, I thought. "And she's living with him," Scott added.

That was it; it was like red rag to a bull. Grandad almost spat his false teeth out on the table and launched into a torrent of abuse about the '*Krauts*' and what they had done during the war and what the hell did I think I was doing in Germany and what was the stupid idea of having one as a girlfriend. It went on and on for maybe five or so minutes. I thought he was going to have a heart attack – poor bloke – he was going a very deep red colour in the face but at last the attack was over and he began to calm down the loony.

Scott was just standing there looking at my grandad with his mouth open. "Time to go I think," I said to Scott. "Yeah," mumbled

Scott. We made our excuses using the ferry as our exit ploy and headed for the door as fast as was politely possible without offending anyone; well, hopefully anyway. "Bloody hell," said Scott, as we drove off in the camper, "What the hell was that all about?" "Well, a wild guess," I said, "Would be maybe the Second World War, don't you reckon?" "Suppose so," said Scott, "But a bit of an over reaction don't you think?" "Yeah, but I know he had a bad time in the army, although that's the first time I've ever heard him talk about any of it," I said. "Bloody hell," said Scott again.

The following afternoon we arrived back at the boatyard. The crossing had been uneventful, and stress and customs free yet again. The weather in Berlin was beautiful and warm; a far cry from the rain and wind in England and as I walked back into the flat, I found Ushi at home. She had taken the afternoon off work and she was very excited when she saw me walk in and said to me, "I've bought you something and also I've bought us something as well!" "What have you bought?" I asked, thinking it might be something useful for the flat, but no, it wasn't at all useful, not in the bloody slightest.

I tried my hardest to look interested when she showed me the twenty one gear mountain bikes she had bought for us, but then when she walked me around the back of the boatyard and pointed proudly to a two seater canoe in a rack and announced this was also ours, I nearly had a baby. And so it began, after working all day on a building site in temperatures in the high thirties and coming home completely knackered, I would find Ushi waiting at the flat, all dressed up in her cycling shorts expecting me to be ecstatically happy about cycling around Tegel Forest or Spandau for two or three hours at a time, without even stopping for a pint or two on the way. I didn't want to rain on her parade but two hours a night peddling a bloody mountain bike around, was beginning to get on my tits, but nonetheless, I thought it was better to humour her rather than upset her by complaining about it. But when the next Sunday arrived, (my only day off) she suggested we took the canoe out for a paddle up and down Lake Tegel. I nearly had a nervous breakdown but eventually agreed to go, what a pair of twats. We came home absolutely knackered; the going had been easy with the wind behind us but paddling back to the boatyard had nearly dislocated my arms from their sockets, we were totally exhausted and spent the rest of the afternoon comatose on the sofas.

As I was lying there slowly dying, I began to think about the reasons I had moved out of the flat with Jackie, Scott and the kids and it kept playing on my mind. I had moved out because it was too crowded, it was too loud, I couldn't sleep properly and I was waking up more tired than I had been before I went to bed! But now my situation was becoming almost the same, I was going to work for ten hours a day, leaving just after five in the morning and returning home at five or six in the evening, then being expected to go cycling or canoeing for two or three hours each evening, followed by a session of bed dancing until the early hours of the morning with Ushi insisting it was quite normal. Quite normal, bloody hell, I was burning more calories after work than I was burning at work. The weight was dropping off me like a stone; I was wasting away to a shadow of my former self. Don't get me wrong, I was enjoying the bed dancing thing but only getting a few hours of sleep a night was beginning to take its toll on me. I was feeling more tired than I had ever felt in my life and I was beginning to look forward to going to work in the mornings to get some well deserved rest!

Work at the race course continued and things were beginning to take shape quite quickly. The new stands were two thirds complete and Scott and I, along with the other brickies, were nearing completion on the first phase of the new buildings on the east side of the race course. It was looking very impressive and the main contractor was using quality materials and sparing no expense on finishes. The end product was going to be very nice indeed as we were just starting to build another footing, Pat walked over and very calmly told us all to get out the footings and walk out of the site as quickly and as calmly as we could because one of the digger drivers had just dug up a World War II bomb and a big one at that. We didn't need telling twice and made our way out of the site to what we thought was a safe distance. Less than twenty minutes later, the police arrived along with half of the Berlin army. The police moved us even further back and closed off the surrounding roads in all directions.

We hung around for over an hour and eventually Pat walked over and said we may as well go home as it looked as if the army were going to try and diffuse the bomb, which would take hours. We were no allowed back into the site to retrieve the camper, so we had to use the S-Bahn to get back home which took bloody hours. The following morning we arrived at work at just before 6am only to find an exclusion zone around the site made of temporary fencing. No one was allowed into the site and Pat, bless him, said he would pay us for the day and then told us to call him later that evening to check on the situation. He also added they had found another two bombs which would probably extend the time to make the site safe again.

We walked back to the station and took the S-Bahn back to Spandau and then a bus back to the boatyard. The journey, which took just forty minutes in the car, took nearly two hours using public transport; it was horrendous. Jackie was on the beach with the tribe when we got home, so Scott and I joined them and spent the rest of the day fishing and swimming in the lake. It was quite nice just relaxing on the beach and not working, and as it was a work day, the beach was almost totally empty. We phoned Pat that evening and also the following two evenings, all with the same result; the bombs were still not safe and the site would be closed until such time as the bombs were made inactive.

By the time Thursday arrived, the site was still closed and we hadn't worked for four days. We couldn't retrieve our tools or Scott's camper, so it wasn't as if we could go looking for another start or go out somewhere without using public transport, which although punctual and reliable, took ages to get anywhere when you used it. Friday rolled around and Scott and I headed for the Irish pub in the Europa centre to meet Pat and pick up our wages. Pat as usual, was three parts pissed when we met him, which was nothing new, so we decided to join him and spent the whole afternoon paying homage to the beer god Warsteiner and by five O'clock, we were babbling bollocks and dribbling in the corner talking to Pat and making absolutely no sense at all. It was great!

At sometime pissed O'clock, Scott and I somehow made the decision to go and get something to eat and stumbled out of the Irish Pub looking for a takeaway on route to the S-Bahn. We definitely didn't want a sausage of any description and eventually found a kebab takeaway in a small backstreet. As we walked in we saw it was run by a family of Iraqis and there was a big picture of Sadam Hussein on the wall in a gold frame with flashing lights all around it. The Gulf War was imminent and was the topic of conversation in the tabloids and also the main topic on the television which we watched on CNN, the only channel we had in English on our televisions at home.

I ordered a donner kebab and Scott ordered a shish kebab. As we waited for our food, we ordered another beer each and stood there waiting for our food to arrive. The picture of Sadam Hussein, which was flashing, kept grabbing our attention and Scott turned to me and said, "Doesn't he, (meaning Sadam Hussein) look a complete idiot all dressed up in his stupid uniform?" "Yeah," I replied, "And he's got a gay moustache as well." The little guy behind the counter, who at the time was cutting the meat for my kebab with a knife nearly two feet long, stopped and turned to us and said, with quite a lot of venom, "Don't insult our leader, he is magnificent, a hero of out time, a man with vision." "What a load of bollocks," said Scott. "Yeah," I said. That was it, he went ballistic and started babbling and shouting at us, and then without warning, jumped over the counter waving his massive knife at us. I grabbed my kebab and we legged it out the shop and off down the road as fast as we could, with the little guy behind us shouting and waving his huge knife. It's already hard enough to run, but its even harder running when you're pissed and can't stop laughing as well. My lungs were really burning and I was finding it hard to breathe, run and laugh all at the same time. As we ran around a corner, Scott grabbed me and dragged me through a door and slammed it shut behind me. It was very dark and as my eyes slowly adjusted to the light, I saw we were in a small pub of some description. We heard the little Iraqi guy run past the door twenty seconds later, still shouting and shrieking something in Iraqi.

We turned still laughing to the bar, and found a rather attractive young blonde woman, standing behind the bar almost revealing most of her assets, and asked her for two beers she plonked them on the bar and said, "That will be 30DM please." "What?" I asked, "30 DM, you're joking." "You get the second beer free," she replied. "Bloody hell," said Scott, "That's expensive!" The first beer didn't touch the sides, and as soon as we had finished them, the bar maid plonked two more in front of us and then asked if we would like to choose something from the menu. "No thanks," I replied and showed her my kebab I was still clutching in my hand. "No," she said, "Would you like to choose something from the menu?" "Just give me the menu," said Scott, "I'm bloody starving," and grabbed the menu from her outstretched hand.

It went very quiet for over two minutes while Scott was reading the menu and then he said, "Take a look at this David, we're in a bloody knocking shop mate!" I grabbed the menu and began to read it. The menu was written in German, English, French, and also polish. It was written as a cocktail menu and began with a pina colada, and next to that written in the four different languages, beginning in German and ending in English, I saw the word blow job. "Shit," I said and carried on reading down the menu. Each drink represented a different sexual act. It was interesting reading and some of the drinks looks quite appealing to say the least!

We had now been in the knocking shop no more than five minutes and I suggested to Scott that we should drink up and make our way to the station. Scott agreed but as we downed our drinks, all these women began walking out from a door behind the bar and made their way over to where Scott and I were sitting. There were eight or ten of them and between them they had on enough clothes to clad maybe one of them. They walked on over to us and we were trapped. They encircled us completely and began grabbing our wedding tackle and making remarks like 'big boy' and other insinuations which were obviously designed to make you feel good about yourself, if you know what I mean.

Scott and I were enjoying the huge complements we were receiving, but I thought it was time to go before we got into a situation we couldn't get out of and started sampling some of the cocktails! So we made our way to the door with the girls in tow, trying their hardest not to let us go. As we shut the door behind us and made our way back up the street in the direction of the train station grinning to ourselves, we heard a scream behind us. We both turned simultaneously and saw to our dismay, not more than 40m behind us, the little bloody Iraqi with the big knife running towards us at a rapid rate of knots. "Oh shit," said Scott, "Not again, let's just do the little git here in the street." "Ok," I said and we both turned to face him, trying to look as menacing as possible as he approached. Forty metres, thirty metres, twenty metres, then as ten metres arrived, a woman pushed a pram out of the shop straight in front of the little Iraqi. He hit the front wheels with his foot and went into a headlong dive and landed on his face at our feet. I stood on the knife and Scott said, "Now, now, who's a naughty little boy then?" The woman with the pram had by now recovered and ran over to the little Iraqi and began hitting him with her umbrella and I mean hitting really, really hard. The poor little guy was now still screaming, but screaming in agony as each blow of the umbrella landed on him. We left her to it and turned and made our way back to the station to catch the train back home and spent the best part of the journey giggling away to ourselves about the whole day's adventures.

I walked into my flat and received my first German bollocking from Ushi. "I took the afternoon off because I knew you were at home and I thought we could spend the afternoon cycling," she began. Result, I thought! Got away with that one, and what do you do? She continued, "You go out with Scott and spend all day drinking and now you're drunk, aren't you?" I offered the traditional reply, "I've only had two beers." That was it, she went totally mental. I saw the book heading towards me but I was in no condition to avoid it. The spine of the book hit me straight in the mouth and pop. Out came my two temporary teeth and landed on the floor. Now it was my time to freak out, but all I could do was laugh about it, after all, it was quite funny and being drunk made it even funnier for some reason. Ushi ran over to me apologising and apologising about throwing the book at me and after a little cuddle, I found myself on the way to the hospital yet again to get my bloody teeth sorted out. As luck would have it, the dentist who had treated me not two weeks previously, was on duty that evening and my new teeth were ready. So, the journey had not been wasted and we left an hour later with my nice, new shiny teeth in place. Hopefully, I thought, this would be my last visit to a dentist to replace my bloody front teeth!

We could not get a hold of Pat over the weekend so yet again we had to use public transport to get to work, which meant we had to leave just before four in the morning to arrive at six O'clock at the race course, and on our arrival we found the site was still closed. The army were patrolling around the site with dogs and entry was still forbidden. A majority of the other lads were also milling around, mostly complaining about not being able to work or retrieve their tools or vehicles. Tempers were beginning to Frey big time. Pat was trying to negotiate with the police and army, trying his hardest to get us into the site to collect our tools and cars but they were not having any of it, no way. Pay could only apologise for the situation and as there was nothing to be done, we made our way back to the bloody S-Bahn and headed off back home yet again. No work meant no money and no money was not acceptable. So, on the way home we stopped off at a builder's merchant and bought some basic German bricklaying tools which were not great tools at all, but would have to do for the short term, and two hours later arrived back at the boatyard.

Our next mission was to get ourselves a job temporarily until such time as we could get back to the race course and continue our work there, so armed with twenty or so phone numbers for various building firms, we headed off up to the phone box and after just two calls, got ourselves a new start for Wednesday morning. This left us the rest of Monday and all day Tuesday to kick our heels. That evening I explained our predicament to Ushi and she simply said, "Why don't you come and work for the company I work for, I expect they need bricklayers?" So the following morning both Scott and I headed off to work with Ushi to meet her boss.

Bernd, her boss, was an ageing hippy with long blonde hair and became an instant friend. He spoke almost perfect English and was a great laugh with it. We spent over four hours in his office looking at drawings of petrol stations which was his and his company's speciality, and also train stations along with housing developments and the odd one off house. It was very impressive stuff and although the drawings were not to the same standard as English drawings, they were fairly straight forward and easily understandable and in some cases, even simple. We told Bernd we were very interested in working for him and asked him what he was prepared to pay bricklayers per day or price work prices per square metre. "Do you not want to work for me as a company?" he replied. "In what capacity?" I asked him. "As a main contractor," he replied. "How would it work?" I said. "You give me a price for the complete job, labour only, and I will supply all the materials," said Bernd. "We wouldn't know where to start pricing work here in Germany," I said. "Well, I'll tell you what I'll do," said Bernd, "I will give you a price and you tell me if you can do it for that price." "Ok," I said, "Sounds fair, and then we can cross check with our prices and see if it's viable for us," I replied. Bernd then went on to explain to us what we had to do as an English Ltd company, to be able to work as a company in Germany for a German architect and construction company. It was fairly straight forward apart from the certification that we needed to get from the Department of Trade and Industry in England. But, he had a telephone number for the DTI in England as he currently employed two or three other English companies and had been through the process a few times already.

We phone the DTI from Bernd's office and received via fax an application form with half a million pages to fill in. It took nearly two hours to complete and after we had finished it, we faxed it straight back to the DTI. The certification process could take up to three months as the DTI had to check all the information we had sent them, just to make sure all the information was genuine and the city in guilds and LTD Company actually existed, and that we hadn't fabricated the application in any way shape or form

"So," I said to Bernd, "We can't work for you yet until we receive the documentation from the DTI?" "Not as a LTD company," he said, "But I can still employ you two as bricklayers if you are interested?"

"Yes," we both said and then I added, "What will you be paying us, per hour or per day?" "40DM per hour," replied Bernd. Scott just looked at me, smiled and winked. "I think you've got yourself a couple of bricklayers," I said to Bernd. "Good," he replied, "Let's go celebrate." So off we trotted to the nearest pub which was handily located opposite Bernd's office. As Bernd was at the bar ordering drinks, I said to Scott, "40DM an hour, that means we will be earning nearly £1000 a week. It's brilliant, another £200 more a week, we're going to be loaded mate!" We were both finding it hard not to jump up and down with excitement; it was a fantastic offer and a fantastic amount of money to earn. Bernd returned two minutes later with three beers, which was the start of a very long afternoon, yet again on the piss!

The next morning, again after not being able to get hold of Pat, we made our way to the race course hoping to be able to retrieve our tools and the camper. We arrived just before six and were pleasantly surprised to find everything back to normal and the site up and running at full tilt again. We found Pat in his cabin and explained to him about our job offer from Bernd and added we would be leaving the Friday coming. "No problem at all," Pat said, "And if you need anymore work in the future, don't hesitate to ring me." That was handy for us to know, just in case things went pear shaped for us with Bernd.

We made our minds up to have a long weekend and actually finish on the Thursday night to be fresh for our new start the following

Monday. It would also give us enough time to go through the prices Bernd had given us and just to check that we could make money on our first petrol station, which we were due to start as soon as we received our certification from the DTI.

Scott was well chuffed to be back behind the wheel of his beloved camper van after being parted from it for over a week. He treated it as anyone else would treat a favourite child and constantly talked to it as we drove home to the boatyard. I had often thought to ask him why he insisted on this practise but after a lot of thought, I had made up my mind not to bring up the subject just in case it caused a major problem of some description, but nonetheless, I was fairly intrigued as to his behaviour. It even went as far on the weekends when he was cleaning it, where he was checking the temperature of the water he was using to wash it to make sure it wasn't too hot! Why? I don't know, but the ritual of cleaning it would take him nearly all day on a Sunday and included a wax and polish, along with the inside being totally cleaned meticulously from end to end. He would cringe if he had to drive it through a puddle in the road and whine about the dust that settled on it if he left it parked on a dusty building site. I think he actually loved the camper even more that Jackie, well he seemed to spend more time with the camper than he spent with Jackie anyway.

As we trundled off home, Scott managed to somehow get us totally lost, which was quite hard to understand as we had been driving the same route for a few months, but nonetheless, we were now completely lost and we didn't even recognise the sign posts which were directing us in all sorts of odd directions, to towns to had never heard of, let alone seen before. We were lost in the old East Germany and a lot of the sign posts didn't actually point to the West German area as they had not yet been updated after the fall or the Berlin wall.

We had seen trams in various parts of Berlin before and this particular town we were now lost in had its fair share of trams, whizzing around in all directions and there didn't seem to be any logic behind giving way to them as there were no traffic signals or give way signs to be seen anywhere. Scott negotiated his way through the town, avoiding trams coming at us from all directions until we eventually arrived at a crossroads, and at last saw a sign showing us the way to Berlin. "Bloody hell," said Scott, "This is doing my head in, all these poxy trams!" I could sympathise with Scott as it was tiring me out as a passenger, watching in every direction at the same time, keeping as eye out for oncoming trams, for Scott, it was ten times worse.

The traffic lights changed to green and off we went, head on straight into a tram which came from the left of us without any warning at all. The tram pushed the camper backwards for maybe five to eight metres before he eventually managed to stop. Scott went totally and absolutely mental, he was out of the camper and screaming blue murder at the tram driver, who just sat in the tram and looked at Scott. This only fuelled

Scott's temper, which was by now escalating to the point of no return. "Calm down Scott," I said, he turned and looked at me and if looks could kill, I would have been dead on the spot. The temper monster now had a hold on Scott and wasn't about to let go in a hurry either. It was time for me to try and diffuse the situation before Scott boiled over completely and did something stupid. He was already punching and kicking the tram, all it needed now was the driver to get out of the tram and the shit would have really hit the fan! Then it happened, the bloody idiot got out of the tram and began to walk towards us, shouting and waving his arms. Scott heard him, spun round and was off. A man on a mission; the mission being to kill the tram driver. Bloody hell I thought, and launched myself off the starting blocks as fast as I could. I knew if Scott got there before me there would be blood and blood in quantity.

As I ran along side of the tram, I noticed all the passengers with their noses pressed up against the windows, watching and waiting for the entertainment to begin. Scott was now behind the camper and less than ten metres from his prey. I took the short cut and jumped between the front of the tram and the camper at full speed. I cleared the bumper of the tram but as I was airborne some three or four feet in the air, I caught site of the two police uniforms walking past the front of the tram towards the tram diver who was still watching Scott heading towards him. I cleared the tram's bumper by maybe five or six feet and hit the two policemen full on. I flattened both of them to the floor and rolled to a stop behind them. Oh shit, I thought, now I'm in the shit big time, really in it. Bollocks! I picked myself up and saw Scott wind up a haymaker and connect it with the chin of the tram driver. He went into orbit and landed flat on his back unconscious some four feet away from Scott's feet.

So there was Scott and I both standing up and on the floor was the tram driver and the two policemen, who shakily picked themselves up after my unintentional flying drop kick, dusted themselves down and began walking towards us looking rather menacing. "I was only trying to stop the tram driver from getting walloped by my mate," I began in my faltering German, but the two policemen were not at all interested in any form of excuse and unceremoniously handcuffed both Scott and I and radioed for assistance which arrived fairly quickly some three or four minutes later. By now the tram driver was back on his feet and feeling brave because of the police being there and launched into a verbal attack on Scott, who although he didn't understand what the tram driver was saying. He had a rough idea and began retaliating with as many swear words as he could muster. The police intervened and led both Scott and I towards the waiting police van. Spandau police station was starting to become a too regular haunt now for both Scott and I, and I was also getting quite concerned with the fact that it didn't seem to matter where we were or what we were doing. We almost inevitably got involved with the police in some way and dragged off to face the music at Spandau police station. For unfortunately being in the wrong place at the wrong time and the more people we talked to, we found a large percentage of them were also being targeted for being English and being arrested for doing something quite innocent in our eyes. But to the Germans' it must have been illegal or a minor offence which ninety nine times out of a hundred, required the perpetrators to be arrested and dragged off to the nearest nick, just for the inconvenience and a bollocking.

As luck would have it, the tram driver didn't want to press charges, so Scott was off the hook and after a short bollocking from the arresting officer, he was free to go so off he went. I sat there waiting for the executioner to arrive. I was not in a cell which gave me a bit of hope, but I had flattened two police officers which was probably assault, so I remained seated awaiting my fate. Eventually after nearly an hour, the two arresting officers walked over to me. God, unbelievably they were even smiling and undid my handcuffs and told me I was free to go. "What?" I said to them. "You're free to go," one of them repeated. I didn't need telling a third time and walked out of the station into the late evening sun. As I walked towards the bus stop, I made a promise to myself to keep a low profile and try to keep both myself and Scott out of Spandau police station in the future by whatever means it took to achieve it, well I could always hope, couldn't I?

Scott had left the police station and gone straight back to pick up the camper. By the time I got home, he was already there wandering around the VW mumbling obscenities under his breath. He didn't look very happy and I couldn't blame him at all. "What's the damage report?" I asked as I walked up to him. Steering rack's buggered, bumper's buggered, front valance and possibly some of the sub-frame is damaged," he replied, "We won't be able to use it for work until it's sorted," he added. We now had quite a large problem, a new job to start the following Monday, which was on a motor way heading towards Hamburg which was not accessible by public transport because of its location, and now we had no transport until such time as we could find a VW repair shop to deal with the damage to Scott's camper. It never rained, it just poured. If anything was going to happen to us in Germany, it always seemed to happen when you least expected it and also happened big time. There were no little problems; they were always absolutely huge problems.

Thursday evenings was 'keep fit night' for Ushi, so both Scott and I retired to Kalle's for a few beers and a chat. For Scott, it was a break from the screaming kids at home, and for me it was just another excuse for another beer or two. "We need to get a car or a van or something," I said to Scott. "Yeah," he replied, "Perhaps Kalle can help us out," he added. After eventually finding Kalle, who was writing a new flyer for the Saturday night Travesty show, he was hiding in a corner so as not to be disturbed, so we disturbed him. Oops.

We explained our problem to him and his reply was, "Just do what I do, and go and lease a car. It's cheap enough here in Germany and easy enough to do. Just decide what car you want and go directly to the main dealer, put two months deposit down and away you go with a brand new car," he said. "Thanks Kalle," I said, and armed with the information, waited for Ushi to arrive so we could hopefully do something about it. Eventually at just after nine O'clock, Ushi walked in Kalle's with her sports bag and still wearing vivid pink leotard which looked rather nice, apart from the sweat, and plonked herself down at our table looking rather exhausted and ordered herself a pint.

I asked her if what Kalle said was correct. "Yes," she replied, "But you will need a bank account to be able to do it." So the next morning, Ushi took the day off and helped Scott and I open a new business account and also a personal account each, and then off we went to the nearest BMW dealer on the Kudamn to find out exactly what a lease vehicle was going to cost us on a monthly basis. It was amazing, to say the least, a 318 BMW with two months deposit down, was approximately £160 a month, so with stupid grins on our faces, we ordered one each as they were so cheap, filled in the paperwork, signed on the dotted line and the salesman said we could pick them up the following afternoon. "How simple was that?" I said to Scott. "Ten times less hassle than in England," said Scott, and then went of to remind me of how long it had taken to get the tipper sorted out back home.

The lease was a simple process but registering the car was a nightmare, an absolute nightmare. Yet again, down to the police station in Spandau along with our paperwork that proved we were registered in Germany, plus a utility bill, our passports and our driving licenses. It took nearly five hours before we left the police station and as Spandau nick was not one of our favourite places at that particular time, it seemed even longer. But at last we got given everything back, all stamped and legal from the police and went back to the BMW dealer to pick up our new toys. I love the smell of new cars; it's great to get something brand spanking new that no one else has driven. It's a lovely feeling and the twenty minute journey back to the boatyard took me over an hour as I had to have a little play with my new toy.

Monday arrived all too soon and we found ourselves heading out of Berlin towards Hamburg at some god forsaken time in the morning, both of us wondering what the new job would bring and was it going to be worth all the travelling just for a bigger wage at the end of the week. But the whole point of coming to Germany was to make money and the quicker we could make it, the quicker we would be able to solve all of our financial problems and return back to England and continue with our lives.

We arrived at the site some ninety minutes later. It was a long way to go in both directions and meant we would be travelling at least three hours each day, but we had made our beds and it was time to lie in it. We found the job and drove in, it was just 6.30 in the morning but surprisingly as we got out of the car, Bernd was already there and as he saw us, he waved and walked over to us. In his hand he was carrying a bottle of schnapps and thrust two glasses into our hands then poured each of us a rather large drink. Not wishing to upset him, we thanked him and chucked them down our necks.

The petrol station had just started, which gave Scott and I a really good chance to see the job from start to finish, which was ideal as we could see the methods of construction and it also gave us the opportunity to find the problems that we might encounter when we eventually started our own job in the future. Bernd introduced us to the foreman and off we went to work, doing what we did best, laying bricks and blocks. The main building was three sided, faced in brick, and the fourth side was the entrance and constructed totally from glass, with an entrance smack bank in the middle. The building was not huge in itself, and the build time was estimated at sixteen weeks from start to finish, up and running.

Bernd was gob smacked. In just under three weeks, Scott and I had finished the brickwork and all the internal block work to boot. We cast the concrete ring beam and then began working on the roof which was very simple in construction and took just a week to complete and with the assistance of the German chippies and was finished apart from the tiling on the roof. Our next mission was to build the carwash which was also constructed predominantly of bricks and was completed in just ten days. Bernd was well chuffed with our work and kept saying he couldn't believe how quickly Scott and I were working and getting things done, but after all, we were doing ten hour days, six days a week, so to us it was hardly surprising at all.

The drainage was our next project and was followed by building the fire breaks between the four huge underground tanks which would hold the petrol and diesel for the petrol pumps. This was very time consuming as each wall had to completely surround each tank to contain any spillage and allow for periodical maintenance. Our last contribution to the petrol station was to lay all the curb edges from the motorway into the petrol station and back out again and then we joined in with the chippies yet again, and spent the next five days pouring all the concrete roads and eventually covering the huge fuel containers in tons and tons of concrete.

Our part of the job was now finished in just nine weeks. Bernd was well impressed with the amount of work we had done in such a short time and took Scott and me along with the girls for a meal to celebrate. We went to Kalle's and as it was a Saturday night, we waited for the trannies to arrive. As we were all eating and drinking, Bernd was talking about Scott and my options for our first petrol station for him as a company. He said currently we could choose from three different locations; one in Berlin, one in Denmark or if we wanted, he also had one in Africa. I just laughed when he mentioned Africa but I saw Scott's face suddenly go from laughing mode to dead serious mode. I knew this look from experience and I also knew Scott had fallen in love with Africa even though his last experience there had been so horrific for him and had nearly killed him. "So, where's this job in Africa?" said Scott to Bernd. I was watching Jackie's face now and I knew exactly what she was going to say, even before she opened her mouth. "You're, or we're for that matter, are not going to Africa. You know what happened last time, I'm not going through anything like that again, so you can just forget about it," said Jackie, now nearly in tears.

I must say it sounded good to me too and Ushi was also looking quite interested as well. Scott would not let it drop and kept asking Bernd questions, the more questions he asked, the more Jackie was slowly beginning to boil over, and when Scott said, "When's the proposed starting date?" Jackie exploded, grabbed the kids and headed for the flat. "Oops," said Scott, "I think I've hit a raw nerve there." "You can't blame her Scott," I said, "It was a worrying time for her and your family; it's not surprising she's reacting like that is it?" "I know," said Scott, "But Africa is such a great place, I would love to go back and see more of it you know, explore a bit and see it properly." "Well, we can't go anyway," I said, "'Cos you went AWOL from the army, I'm sure they would like to see you again, to reacquaint you with army life or prison, don't you think?" "I don't know," Scott replied, "But it would be interesting to find out, don't you think?"

Behind us the trannies were in full blown singing mode and judging by the laughter and clapping, they must have been doing a great job. But we were almost completely oblivious to their antics because we were now so engrossed in the possibility of going to Africa, we hadn't even noticed their show at all. "What about our flats, and what about the fact that we have just leased two brand new bloody cars?" I said to Scott. "We'll take them with us," Scott replied instantly. "So what about Jackie and your kids then?" I asked, "How is she going to react to moving yet again half way around the world?" "Not a problem," Scott said, "Let me deal with that one, I'll talk her round, don't worry about it."

Bernd was very keen for us to take the job in Africa as he hadn't been able to find anyone interested in his offer in Germany, and it was also a great chance for his company to expand outside of Europe. Ushi was also keen on going as she had always wanted to see Africa and work outside of Europe, and if we accepted the job, she would be Bernd's ears and eyes and in control of the financial side of the project.

The rest of the evening was spent discussing the pros and cons of the upheaval to Africa and we also said to Bernd we wanted a written offer regarding the price of the job along with an accommodation package. Bernd didn't bat an eyelid and agreed almost instantly to our demands.

All that remained to be done was to get our certificate from the DTI and to find out exactly how Scott stood regarding his little prolonged holiday from the South African army. This had been over nine years long now and that would have to be the first hurdle to cross before we did anything else at all.

The next day was Sunday and we had all arranged to go fishing for the day, but as Ushi and I were about to knock on Jackie and Scott's door, we heard Jackie screaming at Scott, so we beat a hasty retreat and went bloody riding our bikes around Tegel lake for the day, much to my disgust. At least it was nice and warm, with pubs on the way which cheered me up a bit and made the cycling a little bit more tolerable. I spent most of the day thinking about Scott and Jackie. It was unusual to hear them row and I was worried that it may be something a little bit more serious between them than just a row.

We returned from our marathon cycling tour and headed straight into Kalle's for a beer and something to eat. Jackie and Scott were already inside with the kid eating and drinking. "So what happened about our fishing trip?" asked Scott smiling at me. "Err, um, well we were about to knock this morning when we heard Jackie going into meltdown so we thought we would leave you to it and went on a pub crawl with the bikes around the lake," I said. "Hormones," said Scott, still smiling. "Oh, for god's sake, you're pregnant again," I said to Jackie. "Yes," said Jackie, "And it's twins!" "Oh my god you two are total bloody loonies," I said, "Congratulations to you both." Scott ordered a bottle of champagne to toast the happy news. I dragged up a table and joined it to Scott and Jackie's and the celebrations began in earnest. As Scott and I slowly began to slip into the dribble and babble state of conversation that always followed the drinking of large Warsteiners, the topic of conversation returned to the offer of the job in Africa that Bernd had made the previous day. To my total and utter amazement, Jackie was making agreeing noises about Africa, and I raised an eyebrow to Scott who smiled at me and then said, "Told you so, didn't I?" "So, you're up for it then?" I said to Jackie. "Well, sort of," said Jackie hesitantly. "Well, that's good to hear," I said, "And what is the reason behind this massive u-turn?" I asked. "A better future for us and especially for the children," she said, "It will give them a better quality of life and also hopefully a better education as well, which is more important than anything," she added.

I translated the conversation as best I could to Ushi, who was waiting for me to finish what Jackie had said. Although Ushi's English was slowly improving, it took ages to translate any conversation from English to German or visa versa, but the more I personally had to do it, the more my German language and grammar was improving, which was also quite important to both Ushi and I, and also was fairly important for Scott and I in the workplace. We all now had the same plan, to get to Africa and begin, yet again, a completely new start in a new country. The only two things that were going to stop us now was us not being issued with our DTI certificate, or Scott not being allowed back into South Africa, or even worse still, Scott being imprisoned for going AWOL.

Monday morning, Scott and I wandered up to the payphone so Scott could telephone the South African embassy to find out exactly how things stood between Scott and the fact that he had been 'missing' for over nine years from the army. We thought it best to telephone as oppose to actually physically going to the embassy, just in case they arrested Scott on the spot. I left Scott to it, he was on the phone for over forty minutes and eventually when he came off the phone and began walking towards me, and he had massive grin on his face. "Well," I said, looking at Scott quizzically, "What did they say then?" "They said I was discharged from the army after an unfortunate accident during my basic training," Scott said. "What?" I said. "I can't believe it either," said Scott. "Discharged what a total load of bollocks'. So what does that mean, can you go back into Africa or what?" I asked. "Dunno," said Scott, "The guy at the embassy is going to make some enquiries on my behalf, I've got to call him on Wednesday," he added.

While we were at the payphone, I called the DTI to check on the progress of our certificate, and a very pleasant woman said it had been posted the previous Thursday. I gave the news to Scott as I hung up. "All coming up roses," he said. "Hope so," I replied. As all the signs were now pointing to the possibility that we would be able to go to Africa, we decided to make some enquiries about sending containers to Africa and also to find out whether we could take our lease cars along with us. I called Ushi and asked her to call the lease company to find out if it was possible or not, and Scott and I called some companies in Hamburg that dealt with relocation and container shipping to all parts of the world. Bloody hell, this was going to be bloody expensive to say the least, even a small container was over £2500 and the cars were charged by the length and weight. It was beginning to look like an expensive adventure. Was all the expense and upheaval going to be worth it, I asked myself? Ushi answered that question for us when she arrived home with a written offer from Bernd outlining the price for our first petrol station. We couldn't believe it, the price was unbelievable. "It must be wrong," said Scott. "No," said Ushi, "It's correct!" "Bloody hell," I said, "That's 67 000DM." "It can't be right," said Scott yet again. "It's correct," said Ushi again, looking a bit agitated. "Well it's a lot of money," said Scott, "A lot of money."

The downside was we couldn't take the lease cars out of Germany, unless we changed the lease deal to a 'H. Purchase' deal, which didn't represent a problem, but would cost at least as much again as the lease package. But everything still hung on one thing, could Scott go back to Africa or not, we could not arrange or do anything until such time as Scott had spoken to the guy at the South African embassy on

Wednesday. It took forever for Wednesday to eventually arrive, and when at last it did, we all tramped up to the pay phone together to await the outcome of one phone call that potentially could change all of our lives forever. Scott walked into the phone box, closed the door, inserted a phone card and began to dial the number for the embassy. Jackie and I remained outside, trying our hardest to keep all the kids amused and in one place, while at the same time, trying to listen to what Scott was saying in the phone box. Less than five minutes later, Scott put the phone down, removed his phone car, turned and walked out of the phone box, looking very glum indeed. Jackie and I looked at each other, and then back at Scott. "Well then, what did he say?" I asked. Scott just stood there looking as us. "Come on, spill the beans," said Jackie, shaking Scott by the arm. "We're going to Africa!" said Scott at the top of his voice. All the kids jumped and Chloe burst into tears; once she started crying the rest of them began joining in, one by one the noise was growing by the second. "Now look what you've done," said Jackie, clucking around the children trying to sooth them in a vain attempt to stop them all crying and all perforating our ear drums.

It was now without doubt time to go and celebrate, but before we could do that we had loads to do. We firstly had to formally accept Bernd's job offer, get contracts drawn up and signed by both parties and then get things properly organised, regarding our huge move from

Germany to our choice of new country and brand new life in Africa. Our first port of call was Bernd's office and Bernd had contracts drawn up in English and in German. He took copies of all our paperwork, along with our brand new shiny DTI certificate. It was very exciting now knowing we were soon to be on our way out of Germany and off to Africa.

Bernd's grandmother had left him a house in Johannesburg, which was to be our base, and also our accommodation. Bernd proudly showed us pictures of the house, it was a huge Dutch colonial house and looked absolutely fantastic, with eight bedrooms, a games room and also a large swimming pool. The proposed start date of our first job in Africa was to be August the 10th, which left us less than three weeks to get the ball rolling.

Scott was adamant he wanted to take his beloved VW camper with him, and spent the next two days finding a reputable VW dealer to repair it to the standards that Scott wanted. He wouldn't accept second best for the VW so it ended up costing him nearly £700 to get it fixed. Bloody nutter!

Jackie announced she wanted to go home with the kids to see her family before we went to Africa, which annoyed Scott somewhat, because it cost him a bloody fortune to get them there. Just two days later, they were going which left Scott and I to deal with everything which looking back on it, was probably a very good idea as it happens.

Our biggest problem, believe it or not, was the flat because Scott and I had signed a rental agreement for a two year period, so for the remaining time of the contract, we were going to have to literally pay for it until the end of the term, or if possible find someone to sub-let it which was going to be easier said than done! My flat that I had rented off Kalle, was no problem at all. I told Kalle we would be leaving at the end of July, and he simply said he would refund my deposit as soon as we had vacated the property and he had had time to inspect it for any damage. The only downside was before we moved out; we were going to have to paint it so the next people to rent it had fresh, new shiny paint everywhere. Apparently according to Ushi, it was a common practise and if you chose not to paint the cost of a contractor painting it was deducted from your deposit. So needless to say, we spent the next three days painting the whole flat in brilliant white, which is the standard colour in Germany and not magnolia like it is in England. That done, we painted Scott and Jackie's flat for exactly the same reasons, and by the time we had finished, a week had gone by in the blink of an eye.

Ushi ordered a container, which was dumped in the boatyard two days later and we began to fill it. Bikes, boats, toys, clothes, furniture, tools and a load of junk that we had somehow managed to accumulate without even knowing it. Each item had to be recorded on a customs itinerary that the container company had given us, and by the time we had finished we had over twenty six sheets of A4 paper absolutely packed with all the stuff we were taking with us. Bernd, in the mean time, was also flat out applying for Scott's and my residency and relevant paperwork for his company to employ us. With the help of Ushi and a few others in the office, it seemed to be progressing quite swiftly. The container was picked up the following Monday, along with a promise from the company it would arrive in Africa in eight to ten weeks time. All that was now left to do was for Scott and me to say our goodbyes to all our friends in Germany and get to Johannesburg. We booked our flights for the following Thursday, while Bernd was leaving two days before Scott and I, and Ushi was going to be left to hold the fort in Bernd's office and was going to join us as soon as Bernd returned to Germany. Jackie was still at home with her family for the next ten days and Scott had booked her and the kids a flight for the following week, at some huge sum of money which had really pissed him off big time. It had cost him almost £2500; he was not a happy bunny at all and spent the next two days whining about it.

Our next mission was to get my car, Scott's car and the camper down to Hamburg. Ushi drove my car, I drove Scott's and Scott drove his pride and joy all nicely repaired and shiny again, off down to the same company in Hamburg that were dealing with our container. We dropped the cars off and took a train back to Berlin. That was it, we were finished. All that was left to do was pack our own personal clothes and head for the airport. Scott, Ushi and I had a meal at Kalle's and two hours later, Ushi took us to Tegel airport, and then insisted on getting really upset because she wasn't going to see me for the best part of a month.

Our first flight was to Munich and the second was Charles de Gaul in Paris where we had to wait three hours for our flight to Johannesburg. The luggage went through automatically hopefully, so we had no dramas with customs at all which was quite a relief. We boarded at 8pm and I had managed to get my window seat which meant that Scott was going to have to sit next to whoever had been allocated that seat next to him, and I selfishly hoped he would get what I always managed to get, the big fat boring guy with a life story to tell Scott all the way to Johannesburg. Ten minutes later I was absolutely gutted; this beautiful young blonde plonked herself down next to Scott and instantly struck up a conversation with him. I couldn't believe it, if I had sat in Scott's seat, it would have been a totally different story that I can guarantee without any doubt at all.

I would recommend Air France to anyone wanting to fly to Africa. They are absolutely superb in every way. Food is great along with the entertainment and the seats are excellent, bearing in mind both Scott and I are well over six feet tall, we had no problems with leg room at all. Four feature films, three meals and a few beers later; we landed in Johannesburg and queued up at immigration for our holiday entry visa, as instructed by Bernd, who was dealing with our permanent visas from his office in Germany. Our passports were stamped with our visas, no problems incurred and we trundled off to the baggage hall to reclaim our suitcases. As we found our carousel, our luggage was already there. Now that was quick, very quick indeed. We picked up our bags and headed for customs. We needn't have worried, the customs officers had their hands full with a load of backpackers and we just walked straight through and out into the airport.

I pulled a small map that Bernd had drawn up for us from my wallet, and we headed for the car rental company where Bernd had reserved a car for us. We ended up with a little powder blue Jap motor; it was tiny but it was a wolf in sheep's clothing. Under the bonnet was a 30L V6 engine and it went like a rocket. We pulled out of the airport, me driving, Scott map reading with the tiny map that Bernd had drawn for us to show us the way to his grandmother's house in an upmarket part of Johannesburg called Sandton.

According to Bernd's rather badly drawn map, our destination was approximately between eight to nine kilometres away, while Scott was barking directions at every roundabout and every junction, we made our way slowly through the mid-morning rush hour traffic at a snails pace. You would have through the fact that the traffic was slow, should have helped us in our supposed short hop to Sandton, but no, it wasn't to be. The first place we ended up in was a place called Randburg which looked quite nice from the confines of our car, and Scott was sure we were travelling roughly in the right direction so we continued on still travelling at mid-morning rush hour speed, dead slow and twenty minutes later found ourselves in another area called Centurion. "Scott, this can't be right, we've travelled over twenty five kilometres," I said. "Keep going," said Scott, "And take the next exit on the left." Bloody hell, another twenty or so minutes and we were in bloody Pretoria. It was time to stop and ask directions, so I pulled into a petrol station and asked one of the attendants if he could direct us to Sandton. "Sure thing," he said, "Turn around and follow the signpost to Edenvale at the first robot, then Sandton is signposted from there." I thanked him and jumped back in the car. "What the fuck is a robot?" I said to Scott. "Dunno," said Scott, "Perhaps you misheard him." "Maybe," I said. As we spun around and headed back in the direction, we had just come from, we saw the sign for Edenvale but managed to end up on a ring road which was taking us back towards the airport again, so we elected to head for the airport and start again from scratch.

We had now been travelling nearly two hours and were exactly back in the place we had started from. We studied the map in the airport car park and then again headed off. An hour later we found ourselves, yet again, in Edenvale. Scott threw Bernd's map out of the car window in disgust and let fly with a torrent of expletives. I pulled into the next petrol station, jumped out and walked in. I asked the guy behind the desk if he sold maps for the local area. "Where are you trying to get to?" he asked. "Sandton," I replied. Before the guy had time to reply to me, a voice behind me piped up and said, "I'm going that way, you can follow me if you like son." "That would be very kind of you," I said and walked back to the car to tell Scott the good news. "Result," said Scott.

Two minutes later, the little black guy came out of the petrol station with a can of oil and walked over to a very old Mercedes, which was only just held together with rust. He popped the bonnet and poured the complete can of oil in, shut the bonnet and jumped in. He turned it over and eventually it started with clouds of black smoke pouring out the exhaust behind him. He lurched out of the petrol station with us right behind him eating his exhaust fumes.

We had no trouble keeping up with him because he was driving so slowly, but even if we had lost him, we would still only have to follow the trail of foul smelling black smoke he was leaving in his wake behind him. Some thirty minutes later, he turned suddenly into a side road and a hundred metres later stopped and got out of his car. He walked over to us and I rolled the window down. "Just seen a good friend of mine," he said, "Won't be five minutes," and he wandered off in the direction of four guys standing around a burning oil drum next to some bushes some twenty metres away from us. Ten or fifteen minutes went by and at last we saw the little black guy walking back towards us. "About bloody time," I said. Scott just grunted and stared out the window.

"I'm just waiting for a friend to arrive, he won't be long," he said and added, "Why don't you join us for a beer?" I looked at Scott, "Yeah, ok," he said and we jumped out of the car and followed the little guy across the burnt coloured grass to his mates with the oil drum. "Oh, I'm Ken," said the little guy, suddenly turning and offering his hand. I shook it, "David," I said, "And this is Scott, nice to meet you."

We joined Ken's mates at the oil drum and were introduced to Monty, Darren, Laurence and Scott who all shook hands with us and from a cool box on the floor, came two beers for Scott and I. We sat on a couple of old wooden pallets drinking and chatting away to our new found mates. On the top of the oil drum was a make shift grill and cooking slowly and smelling lovely was some chicken and beef burgers. Ken's mate had still not arrived by the time we had finished our beers, so I asked Ken if there was a pay phone nearby as I needed to phone Bernd, our boss and let him know we had arrived in Africa and would be in Sandton in the not so distant future. "Not around here," he replied, "But you could try the security guard in that building over there, he will have a telephone." I thanked Ken and wandered over towards the building. As I got slowly closer to the building, I noticed the high chain link fences topped with barbed wire, surrounding the huge building. The security guard was very helpful and even dialled the number for me. Bernd answered on the third ring. I explained what had happened and then told him we were lost and were waiting for Ken to eventually show us the way to Sandton. "So where are you now?" asked Bernd. "I don't know, but I could ask the security guard," I added. "I'll ask him," Bernd said, "Give him the phone." I handed the guy the phone and just thirty seconds later, he handed it back to me. "Hi Bernd," I said. "Don't move, stay where you bloody are. I'll be there as soon as I can," said Bernd, "Just don't move," he said again. The line went dead; I handed the phone back to the security guard, thanked him and wandered back off to join Scott at the oil drum.

As I approached, Ken handed me a beef burger and another beer. "Did you get a hold of Bernd?" asked Scott. "Yeah," I replied, "He sounded a bit strange when I spoke to him but he said he knew where we were and to stay put. He was on his way and would be with us ASAP." "That's ok then," said Scott, munching on a huge beef burger. We had now been at the oil drum with our new found friends for about an hour or about five beers and a couple of burgers. We, as far as we were concerned, were having quite a nice time and then all hell broke loose. It started in the distance, the wail of police sirens, it was hardly noticeable to start with but got progressively louder as the minutes went by, and then all of a sudden they were charging up the road just behind us. They came flying up the curb and were heading straight towards us. "Bloody hell," said Scott, "What the fuck is going on?" The four police cars and four vans skidded to a halt in clouds of dust in front of us and all of a sudden there were police absolutely everywhere charging towards us and they were all armed and shouting at us. I couldn't understand what they were saying, but as they got closer, I understood perfectly. "Get on the ground now, get on the ground!" We all complied, including our new found friends. "What the fuck is going on," said Scott to me. "Dunno," I said.

Bernd appeared from the now settling dust and stood directly in front of Scott and me. "You are crazy, English bastards," he said, "Crazy, crazy, stupid fucking idiots." 'What?" said Scott? "Do you know where you are?" asked Bernd. "No," I said, "Not a bloody clue. That stupid map you drew was totally useless; we've been driving around for the best part of five hours looking for Sandton." "Do you know where you are?" Bernd asked again. "No, we don't," I said, as we both stood up. The police had rounded up Ken and the crew and had them completely surrounded. "You are in 'Soweto' said Bernd rather loudly. "Oh," said Scott. "Bloody hell," I said. "It's lucky you're still alive," said Bernd, "Do you know how bloody dangerous it is here?" "Seen it on TV," said Scott. "Yeah, but how were we to know?" I asked. "People get killed here everyday," said Bernd, "Come on, I'll get you back to the house." "Still, we were having a nice time," said Scott smiling at me. "Get in the bloody car," said Bernd rather sternly.

We followed Bernd for the best part of half an hour or so and after driving past the airport for the third time, found ourselves driving past a big sign post saying Sandton. Ten minutes after that we pulled up behind Bernd, who had stopped in front of a huge set of wrought iron gates. Standing next to the gates was a tall thin black guy, very smartly dressed all in black, with a red stripe running down the side of his trousers, and a red collar on his shirt. In his left arm he was carrying an old Lee-Enfield 303 rifle. He punched a four digit number into a key pad next to the gate and the gates slowly began to open. We drove through and parked up next to Bernd and got out. The house was more impressive in the flesh than it had been in the pictures Bernd had shown us. It was absolutely huge and stood in almost a hectare of land surrounded by a ten foot high brick wall with a broken glass set into the top of it along with coils and coils of barbed wire.

"Welcome to your new house," said Bernd, who had by now cheered up a little bit after our little excursion into Soweto. "Bloody hell," said Scott, "It's huge." We stood there awe struck, it was a fantastic place. "Come on in," said Bernd, and we walked into our new home behind him. Standing in the hallway was a huge fat black woman along with another rather large lady and two young lads in their early twenties. Bernd introduced us firstly to Bella the cook, then Clara the cleaner, and then to Bobby and Benjamin the gardeners. Scott and I just stood there with our mouths open. Bernd turned and saw our stunned faces and began laughing. "They came with the house when my grandma died," he said, "And I can't get rid of them as they have been provided for in her will." Oh," I said. Scott just mumbled something and carried on standing there with his jaw flapping open. We followed Bernd around the house as he very proudly showed off his fantastic property. It was beautiful; every room was full of very old but very nice furniture. Each room was beautifully detailed with huge heavy curtains and ceiling fans everywhere. The old gas lamps on the walls had at some time been modernised to accept light bulbs, but the effect still made the house look like a time warp and I felt as it we had just jumped back a hundred and fifty years in time. Oak panel walls filled the reception rooms from floor to ceilings and there wasn't a sign of any modern electrical appliances anywhere, not even a TV to be seen. The kitchen was bigger than the total size of my flat at the boatyard, it was huge and the only modern appliance in the whole kitchen was a massive American style fridge with two massive doors.

We walked up an ornate wooden staircase behind Bernd and walked around the eight bedrooms each with its own bathroom. I chose the third bedroom we went into, with lovely views over the swimming pool and the golf and tennis club which lay opposite the road. Scott decided on the fifth bedroom with a four poster bed in it, and a commode in the corner which was full of paper flowers. Over dinner, which was served in the garden under a rather nice timber gazebo, by Bella and Clara, we sat and listened to Bernd's dos and don'ts in South Africa. It started with the obvious, "Don't go into Soweto under any circumstances," said Bernd smiling at us, "Unless you have a death wish," he added. Scott looked at me and grinned. "It was quite good fun," he said. "Yeah," I said, and we all broke into fits of laughter. We spent the rest of the evening under the gazebo listening to the stories of Bernd's youth and growing up in the house we were now going to be living in. It was very interesting and gave both Scott and I an insight into the goings on in Africa that had occurred over the last forty years or so and also explained why Bernd spoke such good English.

Sleep came very easy that night, as both Scott and I had been without sleep for the best part of forty eight hours. Bella cooked breakfast the following morning and after coffee, Bernd insisted in driving us around the local area of Sandton to show us what was available regarding shops, restaurants, tourist attractions and sporting facilities. The next stop was the proposed plot for our first petrol station in Edenvale. It was just an empty plot with temporary fencing all around it, but was going to be our place of work for the next four months or so. We wandered around the site while Bernd explained how he wanted us to run the job. Now this was news to us because we thought we were only going to be responsible for the brick and block work side of things, and we brought that up with Bernd. "I want you two to manage the whole job," said Bernd, "I will pay you a wage for your time and the price for the brick work and block work is also yours." "Fantastic." I said, "So we will be on the job from start to handover?" "Correct," said Bernd, "And also responsible for organising the labour force and drawing up contracts.

I've itemised the prices for all the labour costs so if you can get the job finished under budget I will pay you a bonus as well." "Bloody hell," said Scott, "It gets better and better."

All of a sudden, Scott and I had a lot more to do than we had first thought and it meant we had only four or five days to find local suppliers and also contractors to cover the work. It was going to be a tall order but Bernd said he had made contact with a few contractors and had sent them copies of the drawings and he was awaiting replies as we spoke. So maybe it wasn't going to be a complicated or time consuming as I had first imagined.

We returned home some half an hour later and on entering the house were introduced to the last member of the household, Walter, the security guard who was seventy three years old but didn't look a day over fifty. He had been working for Bernd's family for forty six years with the same ex-army issue rifle which he cleaned and polished every day. The funny thing was, according to Bernd, he only had one round of ammunition and Bernd said he had had the one bullet since his grandfather had given him the rifle in 1944.

That evening, Scott, Bernd and I went to a restaurant called Giles, which was an old tea plantation house, built into the side of a hill. Half of it was on stilts; the place was great and I knew as soon as we entered, it was going to be a regular haunt for Scott and I as it was less than four hundred metres from 'Halcyon' our house, and they also sold import beers such as Stella. The food was also brilliant but believe it or not, Bernd had insisted that we drove the four hundred metres from the house to the restaurant, just in case we were robbed or assaulted on the way. It seemed crazy to Scott and I and although Bernd had explained how dangerous South Africa could be, we both found it hard to comprehend that such a thing could or would ever happen to us.

Monday began early onsite, meeting with the petrol company's engineer, along with the various different contractors who had tendered for the job. It was a very, very long day and by five pm we had narrowed all the contractors down to just two that provided a competitive price and also a realistic program that fitted in with our program and time scale of the job. They also provided the different trades and professionals to enable us to achieve Scott's and my goal of getting our first job for Bernd finished to program and budget.

Tuesday was spent firstly drawing up contracts and secondly ordering materials from various building merchants in and around Johannesburg. The petrol and diesel tanks had been ordered from Germany and were due to be delivered in two or three week's time. The porta cabins and toilets had also been ordered, along with an electrician to provide temporary power to the site. Bernd was pleased that everything was running smoothly and announced that he would be returning to Germany on Thursday, but before he went he had a surprise for us. "What's that?" I asked. "Well," said Bernd, "We need to take your hire car back to the airport first." "Ok," I said, "And then what?" "I'll pick you up," said Bernd. It was all cloak and dagger stuff and Bernd picked us up from the airport after we had returned the car. We drove for less than ten minutes and turned into a Toyota dealership. As we all got out of Bernd's car, a salesman walked up to Bernd, shook his hand and asked us all to follow him. I looked at Scott; he just shrugged his shoulders at me and said, "Not a clue." The salesman stopped in front of a dark green Toyota Hilux Surf, turned and threw a set of keys at me. "There you go," he said. I looked at Bernd, he smiled and said, "It's a company car for you two to use." I was gob smacked, "Thank you Bernd," I said. "Not a problem, its tax deductible," he replied still smiling. Scott and I jumped in; it was like Thunderbird II inside. I'd never seen so many switches in my life in a car before. The salesman began to explain how everything worked. He started with the gearbox selectors from two wheel drive to four wheel drive, the sunroof, the heated electric seats, how to connect the LPG gas filling hose. It was a huge 4x4 and was brand spanking new. It even had a CD player in it. Wow!

"Now this switch is very important," said the salesman, "It's the anti-car jacking device." "How's it work?" asked Scott. "Jump in and I will show you," the salesman said. We all complied and got into the car. Once the car had started, all the doors automatically locked themselves. "Now that stops car jackers just opening your doors when you're in the vehicle," he said as we drove slowly out of the showroom and into the car park. He stopped the car, and said, "Now this is the last resort switch." "Where?" asked Scott. "This one," said the salesman, pointing at a big yellow switch with a very small skull and crossbones printed on it. "Watch this," he said and hit the switch. I nearly fucking shat myself from the door sills on both sides of the Hilux shot these huge flames about three to four metres. "Fucking hell," said Scott. "Exactly," said the salesman grinning. He then explained there were four gas nozzles each side of the car in the door sills, which ran from the LPG gas that fuelled the car. It was legal at the moment, but was only to be used in an absolute emergency. That was the end of our introductory pep talk regarding the new toy and ten minutes later we followed Bernd back to the house, but not after spending the best part of ten minutes arguing over who was going to have the first drive of our new toy. I won, but only because I was in possession of the car keys.

The next two days, Scott, Bernd and I spent on site working out programs to ensure everything and everybody was ready for the ground breaking the following Monday. Materials had already begun arriving and the site was already beginning to look like a building development. Scott and I built a new manhole and connected the toilet and shower block to the drainage that ran in the main road. The local building inspector arrived out of the blue to check on the drainage connections to ensure they complied with building regulations, and then insisted on checking each and every license that we had received from the local planning department. He was a complete jobs worth, and spend nearly two hours sifting through each bloody document. We were still onsite at after 7.30 waiting for the idiot to finish. At last he said everything was in order and we locked up and headed for home.

Thursday was Bernd's last day in Africa for as it happened nearly eight months, but before Scott and I took him to the airport, we stopped at the site for just an hour and he signed a complete cheque book for us to cover the cost of the contractor's bills along with materials and as Bernd said any unforeseeable problems that might occur before Ushi arrived to take control of the financial side of things. We said our goodbyes to Bernd at the airport, thanked him once again for giving us the chance to prove ourselves to him, and also his trust in us completing the petrol station to program and on budget, and wished him a safe journey back home to Germany.

Friday was D-day for Scott as Jackie was due to arrive that morning along with the kids and without doubt, enough bags and other junk to fill a small skip. We both left the house at just gone 6.30am as the flight was due to land at 6am, and we knew immigration and customs would take at least an hour. It was a beautiful sunny morning and even as early as it was, the temperature was already rising steadily, and as we pulled into the airport car park at just before seven, it was already eighteen degrees Celsius.

The car park was almost empty as we entered and I drove to the nearest point next to the entrance to make life a bit easier with Jackie, the kids and the luggage. I pulled into a free space and leant forward to shut the sunroof. I pressed the switch but unfortunately not the right switch. The switch I had inadvertently pressed was the anti-car jacking last resort switch. The result was as before, instant and also very colourful. The flames as before shot out both sides of the Hilux, hit the two cars parked either side of us, along with two old ladies who were struggling to get a suitcase into the back seat of their car. I had never in my life seen two old ladies in their mid-seventies move so fast before. Bloody hell, they literally jumped out of the flames towards the back of their car. The flame blast luckily lasted less than two seconds and had stopped as soon as I had taken my finger from the last resort button. "Fucking hell," said Scott, as I was jumping out of the car. I approached the two, now smouldering and slightly charred old ladies who were looking, to say the least, a little shocked at what had just happened to them. "Are you ok?" I asked, which was probably a stupid thing to say, bearing in mind what I had just done to them, but it was all that had sprung to mind. "Yes young man," was the reply, "We're fine thank you. Would you mind lifting our cases into the car please?" "Are you burnt at all?" I asked. "No, no, not at all," said the tallest one. "Are you sure?" I said, "It was an awful thing for me to do to you, I'm terribly sorry, it wasn't intentional." "Oh, don't worry about it, it's amazing how resilient tweed clothing is," she said, pointing at both of the tweed suits they were wearing, which as I looked were still slightly smoking, and little puffs of smoke were still swirling around over their heads. I apologised again and then put their two suitcases into the back of their car. They had behaved as if it was something that happened to them every day of the week. I was absolutely gob smacked and as Scott and I walked towards the airport entrance, the two old girls drove by, hooted and waved at us, both of them smiling. "Unbelievable," said Scott. "Bloody lucky I didn't cook them to a crisp," I replied, and that was it, the laughter began and we couldn't stop until we got into the airport complex.

Jackie came through customs and walked into the arrivals area twenty minutes later, with two trolleys, nine suitcases, and five kids all carrying enough toys to fill Toys 'R Us.

The kids simultaneously saw their dad, dropped everything and ran towards him screaming with joy. Jackie looked tired and exasperated after the flight. I climbed over the barrier and grabbed one of her trolleys as she was picking all the kids toys up. Jackie's bump had been growing steadily since I had last seen her some three weeks previously, she looked enormous. Eventually we got to the car but by the time we had squeezed all the nine suit cases into the car, there was only just enough room to get myself into the drivers seat, so Scott had to get a people carrier taxi to ferry his huge family back to Sandton.

Walter was, as usual, standing at the front gate along with his rifle and punched the number into the key pad as we arrived. The kids were out of the taxi in two seconds flat and charging around the garden like headless chickens screaming like banshees. I unloaded all Jackie's and the kids' cases and with the help of Walter, dragged them all into the house. I returned to the car for the last case and as I walked away from the car, I pressed the key fob which locked the car. It was a full closure alarm system but this time nothing happened, it didn't beep, the windows didn't shut absolutely bugger all happened. I pressed it again with the same result, absolute nothing. As I was struggling with the suitcase, I tossed the car keys onto the front seat of the car as I passed the open window. As the keys hit the seat, it went beep, beep and up went the windows. Bloody brilliant I thought, but then I remembered what the car salesman had said to us the day we had picked the car up; there was a spare key in a magnetic box stuck to the back side of the front bumper. I put the case down, lay on my back and edged my way under the front of the Toyota. I felt behind the full length of the bumper, searching for the bloody little box with the spare key. I heard someone talking but I didn't recognise the voice. The next thing I knew was I got the biggest electric shock of my life. Bang, I head butted the underside of the front bumper and nearly knocked myself unconscious. "Fucking hell, that bloody hurt," I said to no one in particular, and grabbed the front bumper yet again to assist me in getting out from under the car. The strange voice I had heard earlier began talking again, but this time, I heard what the voice was saying. It said, "Warning, remove any part of your body in contact with this vehicle immediately; you have three seconds to comply or face an electric shock." Shit, too bloody late, bang, I got another electric shock. It felt as if I was having a heart attack and I'm sure it actually rendered me unconscious for a few seconds or so. The next thing I remembered was Scott dragging me out from under the car by my feet. He was pissing himself with laughter; he could hardly breathe from laughing. "I was watching the whole thing," he said, now almost crying with laughter. "It's the car alarm," he added. I stood up still a bit dazed and slightly wobbly on my feet, blood now running down the front of my shirt from the cut I had managed to give myself head butting the bumper. "For Christs sake, is there anything else I should know about this fucking car?" I said. "You had better let Jackie look at that cut," said Scott, "It looks quite deep mate." Once we got back into the kitchen and as Jackie was cleaning the blood from my forehead, Scott removed a small metal box which was stuck to the fridge like a fridge magnet, and said, "Is this what you're looking for?" still laughing. "Thanks Scott," I said, "So you knew all along I would get an electric shock from the car?" "Yes," replied Scott, "But only because I read the owner's manual," and began laughing yet again. I snatched the magnetic key box from his hand and stuck it back on the fridge door. "I'll get you back somehow," I said, but Scott knew I didn't mean it as by now we were both almost crying yet again with laughter. We introduced Jackie to Bella, Clara and the two gardeners, and Jackie disappeared with Bella to look around her new house. She returned forty minutes later with a huge smile on her face. "It's beautiful here isn't it?" she said, "I love the house and Bella's lovely," she added.

While Bella prepared breakfast, Scott thought it would be a good idea to disconnect the alarm from the car, bearing in mind what had just happened to me and the last thing we wanted was someone else to get a shock, especially one of the kids. So, armed with the spare key from the fridge, we headed towards the garages to look for suitable tools to deal with the alarm. The garage block had three ageing double wooden doors, none of which we could manage to move, let alone open. We wandered around the side and found a door, opened it and began to fumble for a light switch as it was pitch black inside. Eventually, Scott found a light switch and turned on the lights. "Oh my god" said Scott, "Look at this under here." Covered by old dust sheets, black with age, were two very, very old Mercedes cars with German plate's front and back. They were both convertible cars and were in fantastic condition, with leather seats, split screen windscreens, running boards on both sides, huge big lights on the front, and handmade leather cases or travel bags strapped to the back of each car. I looked at the Speedos and each car had travelled less than ten thousand kilometres. This was unbelievable; the cars must have been in the garages for the best part of half a century without moving. There didn't seem to be any rust visible and even the leather seats, although black with dirt, were in almost perfect condition. "I wonder if Bernd knows about these two beauties," said Scott. "Dunno," I replied, "Maybe we should telephone him and let him know," I suggested. "Good idea," said Scott.

Behind the two cars, hanging the full length of the garage was a dirty old blue tarpaulin. We found a gap and pushed our way through it. Along the far wall were three camp beds, a chemical toilet and a rudimentary wash basin. Asleep on one of the camp beds lay Walter snoring gently. He woke with a start and sat up quickly. "Good morning sir," he said. "It's David," I said, "Not sir." "Yes sir," he replied. "No, David," I said yet again. "We're homeless," he blurted out before I had time to ask him anything, "And we've been living here in the garage since the mistress died eight months ago," he said, looking rather sheepishly at us. "There are eight bedrooms in the house," I said, "Grab your belongings and go and choose yourself a room." Walter just looked at us. "Well, go on, off you go," said Scott. "Yes sir," said Walter.

Scott and I returned to the task in hand, picked up a few rusty tools that were lying on an old work bench in the garage and set about disconnecting the alarm in the Toyota. It was quite straight forward and only required the disconnection of a small transformer which was bolted to the inside of the engine bay. We locked the car and tested our handy work by touching the car. "Safe," said Scott, as after ten seconds of touching the car, nothing happened.

As we walked back into the kitchen, Bella and Clara were standing there grinning at us. "Thank you," they both said in unison and then insisted on bear hugging both Scott and I nearly to death. "Well we can't have you all living in the garage," said Scott, "It's not necessary when the house is so big and has so much room," he added. I asked Walter about the two beautiful cars in the garage and he said as far as he knew, until he had actually broken into the garage, the doors had not been opened since he had been working for Bernd's family over forty six years ago. "Bloody hell, so no one even knew they were there?" I asked. Walter and Bernd's family had come to Sandton in the early 1930s and he could remember them even back then because he had worked in the house next door as a gardener. But he had never seen the cars and since he had worked for the family, no one had even driven a car and had used taxis to get anywhere when they needed to.

After breakfast, I called Bernd and told him of our discovery in the garages. He immediately got very excited and asked me to take some pictures of both cars. He said he could remember seeing pictures of his grandparents with the cars in Germany taken before the war and said as far as he could remember one of the cars was a prototype racing Mercedes that his grandfather had bought at an auction in Southern Germany in about 1929 just before the family had moved to Africa. I also mentioned the fact that we had moved all the staff into the house as they had been made, somehow, homeless and had actually been living in the garage since his grandmother had died. Bernd agreed with the idea and then carried on talking about the two Mercedes. "Are the keys in the cars?" he said. "Dunno," I replied. "Do they run?" he asked. "Dunno," I replied. "Can you get them out of the garages?" "Maybe," I said. "I'll make some phone calls and see if I can find a Mercedes dealer or someone to come and have a look at them to see what needs to be done to get them running again," said Bernd. "Ok," I said. "I'll get on with it right now," said Bernd, and click, the phone went dead.

The stress and panic called work began in earnest the following Monday promptly at 7.00am. We had arrived at 6.45 to find ten people already waiting for us to open the gates and as soon as we had done so, the questions began. Where's this, what's that, I need a drawing for so and so, where's the toilets? It was complete bedlam, but after an hour or so it settled down and things began to happen. The petrol station had begun. The petrol company's own engineers of which there were three of them, began by setting up their theodolites all around the site and the rest of their team, another seven, began to peg out with timber profiles outlining the petrol station itself and also the carwash. By the end of the day, there were profiles everywhere, along with site datum's for levels and string lines going in all directions to show the proposed outlines of the roads entering and leaving the petrol station. It was impressive stuff, but Scott and I were redundant. All we could do was stand around and watch them in action. By Friday, the complete site had been set out to the satisfaction of the engineers and they announced they had finished. They said their goodbyes and were gone. It was only midday and just before we locked up the site for the weekend, I called the ground works company and told the contracts manager that we were ready for them to start the following Monday. "Great," he said, "We'll see you Monday then."

That was the end of our first week; it had gone quite smoothly but the weird thing was it had made me more tired just standing around watching than it would have done if I had been actually doing physical work. I was totally knackered and even fell asleep as Scott drove us home. We arrived home some forty five minutes later, drove through the gate and up to the house. "What's going on?" asked Scott. I opened my eyes and saw people absolutely everywhere. "Dunno," I said, rubbing my eyes. But then we saw the Mercedes logo on two of the Lorries and the penny dropped. As Scott brought the car to a stop, we were mobbed by about six guys all asking questions about the two Mercedes. The best thing to do in the circumstance was simply to open the garage side door and let them all in. that shut them all up instantly as they crawled all over the two cars inspecting every nook and cranny. We left them to it and headed for the kitchen, hoping to find a cold beer or two in the fridge.

As we walked into the kitchen, we saw the kitchen table smothered in books and poor David and Millie were sat there listening to this woman droning on about the three times table. They both looked totally petrified and I can't say I blamed them. The woman looked very scary, even to me. Jackie came in smiling and introduced us both to the kids' new teacher, 'Margo' who according to Jackie was going to be teaching the kids five afternoons a week for five hours a day! I felt sorry for both the kids and also for Scott as it must have cost him an absolute packet. In the meantime, the Mercedes guys had managed to completely demolish two of the old garage doors and as Scott and I wandered over to see what they were doing, began to winch the two old cars up into the back of the lorries with an electric winch. The first of the cars moved quite freely into the lorry, the second car's back axle was frozen solid and was digging two trenches in the grass as it slowly disappeared into the back of the transporter. Two receipts were thrust into my hand and off they went, leaving us with piles of wood scattered all over the garden and two trenches halfway across the bowling green of a lawn. Bobby and Benjamin were standing there looking as if it was the end of the world. The gardens were their pride and joy; they were not happy bunnies at all.

Scott and I went back to the house and I called Bernd's office number in Germany to inform him that the two cars had been picked up by Mercedes and were on the way back to Germany via boat. I was surprised when Ushi answered the phone and even before I had time to tell her anything at all, she told me I had to come back to Germany for the next weekend as her brother was getting married and she wanted me there. She had cleared it with Bernd and I needed to arrive no later than Friday. I began to complain about the cost of the flight, the fact that we had only just started the petrol station and we had only just arrived in Africa. The list went on and also my suit was in the container, winging its way to Africa. It all fell on deaf ears; the simple fact was I was going to have to fly back to Germany regardless of what I thought. Bollocks! I was still whinging about it the following Thursday as Scott drove me to the airport. "It's a waste of time going to Germany for just four days," I said. "Yeah, but if you don't go, you are going to get more earache than you ever thought possible," said Scott. "Yeah, I suppose so," I said, and reluctantly got out of the car and headed off towards check in, waving to Scott as he drove off laughing. I had chosen the cheapest option regarding flight costs, which meant returning the same way we had arrived in Africa, through Charles de Gaul airport in France, with a four hour stop over in France and then two flights from France, the first to Munich and the second one to Berlin. Even so, it had cost me over £650 and as the plane took off, I knew by the time I got back to Germany, I was going to be completely bloody knackered.

I landed in France at just before eleven local time and made my way through the maze that is Charles de Gaul to the next departure lounge, and waited and waited bored out of my mind. I hadn't thought to bring anything to read. There was nowhere to get anything to eat and also there was no smoking. The four hour wait might as well have been four days, I was pulling my hair out with boredom and it was a total relief when eventually they announced we could board the flight. As the plane landed in Germany, I noticed it was absolutely pissing down with rain. I had only been gone three weeks, but even in that short time, I had become accustomed to the lovely warm weather in Africa, and I wasn't feeling too pleased to be back to cold and wet rain again. The plane took ages, taxiing to its stand, but I was in no hurry at all as my next flight wasn't due to leave for nearly an hour and a half. Eventually, we disembarked and I headed off towards passport control, standing in line with the rest of the sheep, waiting for some sour faced official to give my passport a quick glance and allow me to pass unmolested.

After what seemed like hours, it was at last my turn. I handed my passport over to Mr, Misery in the glass box. He opened my passport, looked at me, looked again at my passport, and then fed it through the barcode reader and at the same time, picked up a telephone which was on his desk in front of him. A very brief conversation followed and then twenty seconds later, it was without doubt probably the most frightening experience of my life. Not one, not two, but maybe twelve or fifteen heavily armed policemen in bullet proof vests were now running towards me from every direction. A red light began flashing in the ceiling to the left and right of passport control and people all around me were beginning to panic, me included. The police arrived suddenly almost all altogether at the same time. There was no 'hello sir, would you please like to come with us.' Oh no, all I got was someone's knee in my back, followed by a size eleven boot across the back of my neck pinning me to the floor. Then my arms were dragged behind me and I was handcuffed quite roughly and dragged by my arms to my feet. "You've broken my nose, you arsehole," I said to no one in particular, as I noticed all the blood now running down the front of my shirt, and as I watched the blood dripping from my nose and splashing on the floor tiles, I also saw to my horror, my two fucking front teeth lying there as well. Not bloody again. It can't be an unpaid parking or speeding ticket, I thought to myself as I was being literally dragged through the airport. "What the fuck is going on now? I haven't done anything wrong," I shouted. But no one was listening to me at all. The police wanted to get me somewhere and somewhere quickly to boot. As I was frogmarched through the airport, people were just standing and staring at the prisoner, me bleeding all over the place with his long hair stuck in his face and his hands handcuffed behind his back, surrounded by at least fifteen policemen nearly running with urgency trying to get the prisoner out of sight of the general public ASAP.

I felt like shouting out, all I said was that Lufthansa provide crap food, but by now, I was far too scared to make light of the situation I found myself in and I was getting worried as well as frightened, these boys meant business and meant it big time. Not one word had been spoken to me and no one had even answered any of my questions. We were still nearly running through the airport when, without warning we rounded a corner and went charging through a double door with security in big red letters written over it. Then we crashed through another set of double doors and into a holding area. This I knew because both sides were lined with cells and most of the doors were open. I noticed as I was pushed backwards into a cell and promptly fell on my arse on the concrete floor, the door banged shut and all of a sudden it went quiet, very quiet.

What the fuck in going on, what have I done or more to the point, what do they think I've done and why is no one speaking to me? I sat there pondering the reasons for my incarceration until suddenly I remembered my mobile phone was in my jeans pocket. I struggled for the best part of five minutes trying to get my phone out of my front pocket, almost dislocating my shoulder in the process. Eventually I managed to turn it on and by leaning against the wall I could just managed to see the key pad. It was hurting my shoulder and my cuffed wrists forcing my arm across, but at least I could see what I was doing. I called Bernd's office; it began ringing and continued ringing until the answer phone picked up. I left a message telling Bernd I had been locked up at Munich airport and needed help ASAP please! I then scrolled through and found Ushi's number and pressed dial. It took ages to connect but after what seemed like hours she answered. I didn't give her a chance to speak and quickly told her what had just happened to me and where I was. I was on my knees; the phone was lying on a wooden bench in front of me. I had my ear pressed against the phone talking when all of a sudden the telephone slipped between the wooden slats and fell to the floor. It hit the floor and pop, off came the back and the battery slid right under the bench. I had absolutely no hope of reaching it at all with my hands cuffed behind my back. At least I thought I had managed to get hold of Ushi. Now all I had to do was sit back and wait for the cavalry to arrive and blow the doors off and get me out. Good plan or what?

I was just thinking to myself that I wouldn't want to be the policeman that picked up the phone when Ushi called. When my cell door flew open and in walked two huge gorillas grabbed me under the arms and literally carried me out of the cell. The fear and panic returned instantly and I began to get very frightened yet again. The silent treatment continued as I began complaining to my two captors, neither of them even looked at me let alone would answer me. I half walked and half stumbled out of the airport and was unceremoniously thrown into the back of a large seven series BMW. The two gorillas jumped in, one either side of me and we sped off at warp factor eight heading for the motorway and Berlin, which was some eight hundred kilometres north east of us.

As I slumped in the back of the police car, I began to try and think to myself what could possibly warrant the reaction for what was going on. I hadn't been arrested; I hadn't even been spoken to. Perhaps it was tax evasion I thought, or maybe I just fitted the description of someone who had committed a serious crime again. Oh well, I thought, there's nothing I can do about it until I know what I'm supposed to have done. The driver, I noticed, was travelling at nearly two hundred kilometres per hour, so he was definitely in a hurry and we were definitely heading towards Berlin.

I don't know how I managed it, whether it was the fact I was tired from travelling or maybe the droning of the car tyres on the motorway, but somehow even as stressed out as I was, I managed to fall asleep. The sound of the car door slamming woke me up with a start. It was pitch black and the car was still running. I looked out the window. For fucks sake, we were outside Spandau nick again. There was just no escaping this bloody place. Two minutes later, I was dragged out of the car and into Spandau nick. It was now nearly one O'clock in the morning and the deck Sergeant was looking rather tired. It must have been a long day and the last thing he must have wanted at this time of the morning was me standing in front of him. By now I was almost professional in the process that followed; uncuffed, pockets emptied, stripped bollock naked, cavity search (how nice was that?) and then thrown into a cold ceramic tiled cell, door slammed and sweet dreams. At least this time they had not cuffed me to the wall rail and I could lie down on the hard wooden bench. Sleep arrived at some time but I slept erratically and kept on waking every twenty minutes or so.

Morning arrived and all the lights came on. A shrill alarm sounded from a speaker in the ceiling somewhere and ten seconds later my cell door opened. Room service had arrived with my breakfast; how nice was that? I took the tray from a very large, no; let's get it right, a huge fat bloody German woman police officer who looked like she had been chewing a wasp for a while. She slammed the door shut behind her and left me to my breakfast. Breakfast? Nah, it looked like something I would feed to a dog. It was all sloppy and running with what looked like gravy, maybe. As before I chose not to eat it and instead just drank down the mud that was supposed to be coffee. Boredom set in and I began counting floor and wall tiles again. That didn't take long then I saw two house flies and spent ten or twenty minutes watching them doing what flies do. How sad is that, I hear you say? Time passed, I don't know how long I sat there as I had been deprived of my watch yet again. But then I heard the key turning in my cell door and it opened quite slowly revealing Mr. Bad English and his side kick, Mr. Bad Breath. I nearly burst out laughing but managed to stifle it somehow.

They walked in and as before cuffed me either side of them. "You come with us now," said Mr. Bad English and off we went out of the cell and towards the lifts up the corridor.

In the lift was a mirror filling the whole side of the back wall. I looked at my reflection; I looked terrible, dry blood all over my face and down the front of my shirt. I opened my mouth and saw the two stumps where my teeth had been knocked out. It looked like I had done ten rounds with Mike Tyson. My eyes were beginning to turn black from the bruising where I had hit the floor and my nose was crooked to one side where it was broken. A picture of health I thought to myself, lovely. We walked from the lift into an interview room opposite and as we walked into the room, I saw Bernd sat at a table with another guy I had never seen before. He stood up as we walked in. "Are you ok?" asked Bernd. "What does it look like?" I replied. "Bloody hell," said Bernd, as he saw the blood on my shirt and my two stumps, but at least I thought Bernd was there, one friendly face among the hostile Berlin police.

Mr. Bad English told me to sit. I complied and was handcuffed to the metal table. "Bloody hell," said Bernd again, looking at my face, "What happened?" I quickly told him what had happened after landing at Munich airport. "Fucking hell," said Bernd after I had finished, "You look awful," he added. "Thanks," I replied. "This is Dieter," said Bernd, "My best friend and also a lawyer." Dieter stood up and went to shake my hand but then realised I was cuffed to the table and sat down again. "Hi Dieter," I said, "Nice to meet you." "Unfortunate circumstances," said Dieter, in perfect English, "But yes, it's nice to meet you too." "So," I said to both of them, "What the bloody hell's going on, what the hell have I done? Why am I being treated like a criminal?" "DRUGS," said Dieter, very slowly enunciating every letter. "What, you're fucking joking," I said, "I never have had or never will have anything to do with drugs!" "That's what you've been arrested for," said Dieter. "No one has said a word to me, let alone arrested me," I replied. Dieter began making notes in a pad he had on the table in front of him, making tutting noises as he did so.

Mr. Bad English and Mr. Bad Breath plonked themselves down at the table opposite me with a tape recorder and the interview or interrogation began. Bernd was acting as translator as the conversation in German was too fast for me to keep up with. "So," said Bernd, "Where did you get the plants from?" "What bloody plants?" I asked. "The plants in your flat," said Bernd. "Don't know what you're talking about," I said. "The six hundred and fifty plants and the hydroponics system that was discovered in your flat by your landlord last week," said Bernd. "Nothing to do with me, we moved out and sub-let it over three weeks ago. You already knew that Bernd," I said. "I'm only translating what this idiot said," Bernd replied. "Oh, yeah sorry," I said. Bernd continued translating what Mr. Bad English was asking. "So, who did you sub-let it to?" asked Bernd. "Two English guys called Simon and Ray," I said.

The penny finally dropped. Scott and I had talked to Simon and Ray and asked them if they had wanted to sub-let our flat. They had readily agreed as it was furnished and relatively cheap, plus it was also in a nice area with good access to most of the construction sites in and around Spandau. The pair of wankers had turned it into a skunk weed factory and now because I suppose Scott and I held the rental agreement, the police thought I or we were responsible for the drug factory. Wankers!

"I can clear this up in two minutes," I said to Bernd. "How?" asked Bernd. "Well," I said, "Ushi made Scott and I do the proper legal thing regarding the sub-letting and made us fill in a legal form she had downloaded from the internet, and both Scott and I had signed it along with Simon and Ray. She said it would protect us from Simon and Ray if they defaulted on the rental payments. "Brilliant, brilliant," said Dieter, "This is ALL you need to prove to the police that you are not responsible. Where's the document?" "In the container on its way to Africa," I replied. "Shit, without it you're fucked!" said Dieter. "Fantastic," I said, "So what happens now," I asked Dieter. "You will be formally charged and then incarcerated until such time as a date for the court hearing is booked." It was getting better by the minute, I was beginning to boil up and about to explode, but what could I do? Not a bloody thing. I was in a police station handcuffed to a metal desk. I was bollocked until I could prove my innocence and in Germany, I was guilty until proven innocent. I was fucked and fucked big time!

"I will get on to the shipping company," said Bernd, "And try to find out if we can get hold of the document before the ship docks in Africa. I will also see if I can arrange bail for you." "Thanks Bernd," I said, and then added, "Sorry about all of this." "Not your fault," said Bernd smiling. As I was having my fingerprints taken, yet again some twenty minutes later, I was thinking to myself how I was going to kill Simon and Ray for what they had done to me and it began to cheer me up a bit as all the methods of their slow and painful deaths kept popping into my head. But my pleasure was short lived as ten minutes later I was escorted by Mr. Bad English and Mr. Bad Breath out of the police station and into the back of a windowless police van that was waiting outside for me.

The journey was only a very short one, and five minutes later the back doors opened and we got out of the van. We were still in Spandau I noticed, but on the outskirts. I knew where we were as Ushi and I had quite often cycled pass the prison on the way to a small pub we had sometimes used in the forest behind it. Now prison was going to be a new experience for me and as we walked up towards the main entrance, it suddenly became very, very clear to me that this was a very serious situation. I was going to be locked up in a bloody prison, in a cell, on my own, or probably with a mass murdered or someone equally as dangerous or obnoxious, or even violent. The prospect didn't make me feel too happy about my immediate future, not at all! It wasn't fair. I hadn't done anything wrong, it was not my fault I was here, and I decided whatever penalty I had to pay for other peoples' misdemeanours would, on my release, be paid back ten fold and with malice, that I could guarantee without any doubt at all. Fucking wankers!

As I was marched up towards the main doors, Bernd and Dieter appeared from nowhere and Dieter asked me if I had a phone number for either Simon or Ray. "Yes," I said, and all of a sudden it got my hopes up. "Trouble is," I said, "My phone is in pieces somewhere on the floor in the holding area at Munich airport." "We'll get on it immediately," said Dieter as I was dragged through the main doors. "Thanks," I managed to say quickly before the doors shut behind me, and left me cut off from the rest of humanity. My introduction to incarceration began in much the same way as being arrested had. Mr. Bad English dumped all my belongings on the desk in front of me and then we went into the same routine as before. "Remove your clothes," said Mr Bad English. I was now sure this sadistic sod enjoyed the process as did Mr. Bad Breath. I was just hoping I wasn't about to receive another cavity search, when in walked a woman police officer who was calmly putting on a pair of latex gloves. Oh bollocks, I thought, how pleasant is this going to be? The unpleasantness was now over and done with, thank god. It was now time to enter the prison which was quite a complicated affair of three security doors made of metal. We passed through the first one which shut loudly behind us, then a buzzer sounded and the second door opened in front of us. As before, we walked through and clang, it shut solidly behind us. Next the buzzer sounded again and the last door slid slowly open revealing yet another desk with three uniformed prison officers behind it. They looked almost as happy to see me and the two goons, as I was to see them. They were all typical Germans, cropped flat top hair cuts, silly peaked caps much like the police force issue, and uniforms pressed so well you would probably cut yourself on the razor sharp creases. Oh god was I going to enjoy being locked up in here. Thoughts of the suffering I was going to reek on Simon and Ray kept popping into my head again as I was being barked at in German by one of the prison officers. "Where's your passport?" he shouted at me. "How the hell should I know?" I replied. "Passport," he shouted again. I chose to answer this time in English and told him to fuck off as loudly as he had shouted at me. "You speak to me in German," he said. His mouth so close to my nose, I could tell what he had had for breakfast. I thought about it and common sense suddenly stepped in to the equation and I thought it may be a very, very good idea not to upset this giant of a man just in case he turned out to be an important cog in the wheel.

In the meantime, Mr. Bad English and Mr. Bad Breath had made their exit, returning through the three security doors and back outside to rejoin the rest of the human race. I unfortunately had to remain inside now watching the goons systematically sifting through my wallet, placing my driving licence, credit cards and a string of receipts on the desk in front of them in a vain attempt to find something incriminating I suspected. I stood there for maybe twenty five or thirty minutes watching them pushing my belongings from one end of the desk to the other until at last they got bored with the obviously important task of getting information from my bits and pieces and decided to escort me off down a long corridor through another metal security door and into the prison complex.

As the last door opened slowly, I was trying to look past the two goons to see exactly what awaited me. To my surprise as the door fully opened, it revealed a social area more appropriate to a hotel. It was full of 'prisoners' playing snooker, darts, card games and also watching TV. This didn't look too bad, I thought to myself as I was marched through the social area and off down a long corridor with doors each side. Each door was numbered, odds on the left and evens on the right. The goons stopped outside door number seven, removed my handcuffs and opened the door. "Your room," said one of them as he walked off leaving me to it. At least I had a room of my own. I saw as I looked around my new cell, to the left was single bed and a small bed side cabinet, on the back wall was a wardrobe and in the corner was a wash basin. It was very, very basic but a lot better than I had imagined. The only clothes I had were the ones I was standing in as I hadn't even got past passport control, let along got to the baggage carousel to retrieve my case at my Munich airport. I had no toothbrush, no clothes, and no soap and also as my wallet had not been returned to me; it meant no money to buy anything. Not even a pack of cigarettes and as the nicotine monster was now driving me up the wall, I decided to make tracks to the social area and try and bum a fag.

As I walked back up the corridor towards the social area, I began to hear different languages being spoken. French, Turkish, German and thank god, also English. I headed for a corner next to the dart board where most of the English seemed to be standing together playing darts and chatting. As I was about to say hi and introduce myself, I heard my name being called. I turned around to see who it was and saw Mark and Mickey, the two scoucers with the brand new Jaguar I had met in Berlin on Scott's and my first visit to Germany, both standing there grinning at me like two Cheshire cats. "Bloody hell," said Mark, "What the hell happened to you?" I spent the next hour explaining what had happened to me once I had landed at Munich airport, all the while smoking their cigarettes which were great, as I hadn't smoked since I had been on the way to the airport with Scott which now seemed like days ago. "You need to get your nose and teeth seen to as soon as possible," said Mickey, and told me to follow him to the medical unit.

I couldn't think of anything better as every time I breathed in, my nose was killing me and if I breathed through my mouth, my teeth were killing me too. It was a no win situation and I was glad to walk in to see the doctor, who immediately set about manipulating my nose back into shape. It hurt like hell, but at least it was now straight again. I then had to wait over two hours to see the dentist who then cleaned my two stumps and fit me with two very roughly made temporary teeth. The job done, I returned to the social area and found Mark and Mickey. It was my turn now to find out how these two had managed to end up in prison; as if I couldn't have guessed.

I was wrong, completely wrong. I had thought it must have been something to do with the selling and re-selling of the Jaguar, but as it happened, they had both been imprisoned for breaking and entering, the idiots. They had been thrown out of their digs for not paying their rent and in a drunken stupor, had broken into the house to retrieve their passports, clothes, and other belongings, only to be arrested at the scene and giving ninety days for their trouble. It didn't seem to bother either of them in the slightest, to be locked up and Mickey even found it quite amusing for some peculiar reason. But for me, it was a relief to have two people I already knew to help me through what may have been quite daunting on my own.

Bernd and Dieter paid me a visit along with Ushi on the Tuesday afternoon, by which time most of the bruising had come out across my nose, and both my eyes were also a lovely shade of yellow and black. Ushi was horrified to see me looking such a mess, but I had to remain separated from all of them by a glass screen across the middle of the table. It was only about a foot high, but neither of us was permitted to pass anything across to each other. Bernd had retrieved my passport and my baggage from Munich airport, which meant at last I had fresh clothes and toiletries and he said he had also put 1000DM in my case so I could buy what I needed from the prison shop. Dieter had also spoken to the shipping company only to be told that even if they could find the document, they had no way of sending it back to shore, so until the ship docked in six weeks, I was just going to have to sit stuck in prison until the rental agreement was faxed back from Africa to prove my innocence. Bollocks and double bollocks!

There's no news like bad news but it was about to get worse. The visit was firstly restricted to just thirty minutes and after the visit we had to go through the whole 'get naked businesses and 'finger up the bum' treatment yet again. I was getting more than pissed off with this bloody stupid, sadistic German policy and hoped I wouldn't be getting too many regular visits a week as I knew I couldn't take too much more of this. Not only was it degrading, but it was also bloody painful. No, fucking painful!

Wednesday arrived and to make the perfect end to the day, so did Ushi for a visit. For fucks sake, I was going to have to nip this in the bud or I was not going to be able to sit down for a fortnight. She was quite hurt at first when I said she would have to restrict her visits but when I explained to her the reason for it, was she concerned? No, she spent the next ten minutes crying with laughter. She thought it was bloody hilarious. I wasn't amused but her laughter was infectious and the next thing I knew we were both pissing ourselves with laughter. I don't know why, because I knew when she left I would definitely not be laughing at all. The prison officer announced the thirty minutes were up and as Ushi left I reminded her to also tell Bernd and Dieter to try and keep the visits to a minimum and only come if it was absolutely and completely necessary. I could still hear her laughing as the door closed behind her.

Two weeks dragged very slowly and no one had paid me a visit. I didn't know what was worse, not having any visits at all or having an appointment with Mrs. Latex finger. I was still weighing up the pros and cons of the visit against the latex finger, when one of the prison officers came up to me and told me I had visitors. I followed him down to the visitors' rooms and was escorted inside and as before, was told to sit at the table and keep my hands behind the glass partition at all times, or the visit would be terminated. Two minutes later, in walked Bernd, Dieter and Ushi and sat opposite me on the other side of the table. "So how's it going?" asked Bernd. "Not too bad," I replied, "But I am getting a bit bored. There's only so much snooker and darts to be played before it drives you totally mad." "Well," said Dieter, "Let's get down to business." Out of a briefcase he pulled a small file, "Your court case has been booked for Monday in two weeks time and as the ship is not due to dock in Africa until the following week after that, we are going to ask the judge for a stay." "So what does that mean?" I said. "Well," said Dieter, "We will all go to court in two weeks time and say to the judge that we need another week to prepare your defence and then we explain to him about the situation regarding the ship and the rental document and then we hope he gives us a week or ten days to allow us to get a copy of the document to prove your innocence." "Ok," I said, "So it all boils down to whether the judge will give us time or not?" "Basically that's it," said Dieter, "But we are just going to have to wait and see what the outcome is." "Fantastic," I said sarcastically, "So what happens if we don't get the time to get the rental agreement back to the court?" "You will probably be found guilty and sentenced to a minimum of five years," said Dieter. I was so shocked over what Dieter had just said, I was totally speechless. "Five years," said Ushi. "Yeah I heard the first time," I said. Now this was serious and I began to panic. "You must try and find Simon and Ray somehow," I said to them all, "Go to all the Irish pubs and ask around. Try and find out where they are and get the information to the police ASAP." "What do you think the police and us have been doing for the past two weeks," said Ushi. "Oh sorry, I didn't realise," I replied. "We are all trying as hard as we can to find anyone who knows where we can find them," said Bernd. "Thanks," I said, and then added "Sorry again." I really meant it as I hadn't realised how hard they had all been working behind the scenes to get things moving in my favour.

The prison officer began to tap his watch with his finger and I knew that my time was unfortunately up. Bernd, Dieter and Ushi stood up and said their goodbyes. Ushi blew me a kiss and told me to keep calm and under no circumstances to panic. 'Keep calm,' bloody hell, how in god's name could I keep calm? I thought it sounded to me, after speaking to Dieter, that I would probably be spending the next five years just playing snooker and darts, paying the penalty for Simon and Ray's crime. I was not a happy bunny, not at all.

As I was escorted out of the visitors area, and off towards my next appointment with the sadistic bitch and her latex gloves, I began to imagine to myself how I was going to cope with five years stuck in this bloody shit hole, with shit food, crap TV in German only, only snooker and darts to keep me occupied. I was going to go stark raving mad; I would be a complete vegetable by the time I got out. I had now been in prison for a total of just nineteen days; how would I feel in a thousand, eight hundred and twenty six days time?Or five years in English.The thought of this began to drag me down, I was beginning to get very depressed and the more I thought about it, the worse I became. As I walked back into the social area, it became even worse. Walking towards me with two suitcases was Mark and Mickey, their ninety days duly served and they were on their way back into the land of the free. We had a very brief conversation as they were both itching to get out of the shit hole. They wished me good luck and also very kindly said they would do their utmost to find Simon and Ray or at least try to get some information as to their whereabouts if at all possible. I thanked them for their kindness and that was it. They were on their way out via the three electric metal doors, accompanied by two prison officers. As the first door closed behind them with a loud bang, all I could think of was what a pair of lucky bastards. Now I was on my own, apart form two other English guys, one who I had not even bothered to ask his name or introduce myself to as to be quite honest, he scared me and looked more like he might be more interested in killing me as oppose to talking with me, and then there was also Graham, the other English lad. Graham was a complete anorak and spent all day, every day doing jig-saw puzzles and talking to himself, or laughing out loud at nothing. He also had a nervous twitch which made him wink a lot. A very worrying individual indeed, so needless to say I kept my distance from the pair of them. This left me no one to talk to unless I wanted to talk with the German lads, but the way I was feeling I really couldn't be bothered to go to all the effort and threw myself into playing darts and snooker on my own. Sad bastard, you reckon? But put yourself in my shoes, I bet you would have probably done much the same thing. I was by now totally bored beyond belief and the time wasn't even dragging by slowly. Time, it seemed to me, had somehow slowed down and as each day passed very slowly, it felt more like two days or even three.

The Monday of my court case eventually rolled around to my relief, and it felt to me as if I had already served a life sentence. I was handcuffed and taken through the three metal security doors and placed into the back of a waiting police car flanked by two police officers either side of me and off to the court house in Spandau. I was met at the court house by Dieter, Bernd and Ushi, all dressed in suits. I was standing there in a pair of tatty old Levis and a t-shirt; they made me feel a bit out of place, but it would have to do as it was all I had to wear. We sat outside the court waiting to be called, all the time Dieter was talking to me, letting me know exactly what was going to happen and exactly what to expect when we eventually got into court to see the judge. We sat waiting patiently for nearly an hour and then all of a sudden we were called. I began sweating as we walked towards the very imposing floor to ceiling wooden doors. Dieter saw my apprehension and told me not to worry as he would be doing all the talking, and if the judge happened to want to ask me any questions, Bernd was on hand to deal with the translation for me, and would be sitting next to me to let me know exactly what the judge was saying. "Thanks," I said to Dieter, but I was still bloody worried and as we walked into the courtroom, for some reason I began to think the worse.

As it happened, it was a very informal meeting, with only the judge, a stenographer and the four of us. It took less than three minutes and before I knew it, we were on our way back out again. "Good," said Dieter, as he closed the door, "He's given us a week in which to provide the document in a view to clearing you from the allegations." It was as if a weight had been lifted miraculously from my shoulders and I suddenly found myself feeling a lot happier about the whole thing. We all sat outside the courtroom as Dieter explained to me what had been happening over the past two weeks. "It seemed as if Simon and Ray had either left Germany by driving across an unmanned border because if they had flown or used a ferry from Hamburg they would have been arrested on the spot, or they had moved from Berlin to another city. It was not important," said Dieter, "As long as the rental agreement you and Scott made with them carries their signatures and passport numbers, you will be found automatically not guilty." "Fantastic," I said, because I knew the document had both their signatures and their passport numbers on it but only because Ushi insisted that we had made the whole thing legal. I looked at her, smiled and said, "Thank you." "You're welcome," she replied, grinning at me.

Bernd suddenly gave me his mobile phone. "Hello," I said. "Don't bend over in the showers," said Scott and burst into a fit of laughter. "Piss off you wanker," I said and erupted into laughter myself. "It could only bloody happen to us," said Scott, when he eventually stopped laughing. "I know," I replied, "But Scott you must, before you do anything, find that document and fax it to Bernd's office as soon as you can mate, or I will be right in the shit!" "Yeah, no problem," said Scott, "The ship is due to dock in five days time, I'm going straight to the docks as soon as they phone me." "Thanks mate," I said, "I just want to get out of Spandau and out of Germany ASAP." "I understand completely," said Scott, "I'll be right on it as soon as I get the call from the customs handlers."

After my very brief taste of freedom, which had lasted less than two whole hours, it was unfortunately time for me to return to my nice Spandau hotel. I thanked Dieter, Bernd and Ushi for their help and said I hoped to seem them all in a few days' time after Scott had found and faxed the document to secure my release. I returned to the prison in a very good mood. I now knew that I had only a very short time left before I was proved beyond doubt innocent of the allegations and released back out into the normal world.

How the hell can five bloody days take so long to go by? I don't know but each day just seemed to stretch itself out and kept on stretching itself out until each and every day seemed to last a week. I was pulling my hair out and in the process, winding myself up to the point of exploding on the spot. Friday night was the absolute worse time of all. I felt like a little kid waiting for Christmas day morning to arrive so I could open all my presents. I was going mad lying on my crappy little bed, just trying to get to sleep. The harder I tried to sleep, the harder it became to actually go to sleep. Each time I looked at my watch, just five or ten minutes had elapsed. Argh! It was no good; I wasn't going to sleep so I got up and sat on my bed reading a book I had managed to borrow from Graham. It was all about steam engines, very boring unless you're a steam engine fanatic, but at last 7.30 arrived, the buzzer sounded, and all the cell doors automatically unlocked themselves. I was out and off down the corridor before the buzzer had even finished buzzing. I was first in the mess room for my breakfast and by eight O'clock, I had almost overdosed on coffee.

Come on Scott, get into that bloody container and find the rental agreement and fax it to Bernd mate. I want out of this shit hole right now. I was willing for someone to phone the prison and say everything was in order and to release me. It was so frustrating not having access to a phone, to find out exactly what was going on. I was tormenting myself just thinking about it. Graham walked over to my table carrying a tray with his breakfast on, and made the very bad mistake of saying good morning to me. Poor bloke. I just ripped his head off and told him to leave me alone. He did a quick u-turn and plonked himself down at another table, looking a bit flustered with my outburst. But two minutes later I noticed he was back to his normal self and chatting away happily to his breakfast, totally oblivious to all the eyes watching his strange behaviour. It made me wonder just exactly what he had done to warrant being imprisoned. Maybe he was just a harmless lunatic. I didn't know, but thinking about the possibilities kept me amused for a while.

At last, just before 2.30pm I felt a tap on my shoulder. I turned around and was told by a prison officer that I had a phone call. About bloody time I thought as I followed the officer towards the visitors' area, and into the prison wardens' office. He motioned for me to pick up the phone. I grabbed the phone, "Hello," I said. "Hi David, its Bernd," came the voice on the other end. "Hi Bernd have you got any news?" I asked. "Yes," said Bernd, "We are at the court house right now, waiting to see the judge and get your release signed." "Fantastic," I said, "So I will be out of here today?" "Dieter and I will be up to pick you up as soon as we can, so pack your stuff and be ready." "Great, I will see you soon," I said and hung up.

Two hours later, I was walking out of prison with my small suitcase and the biggest smile in the world on my face. I was met by Bernd, Dieter and Ushi. "Thirty nine bloody days," I said as I walked towards them grinning like a Cheshire cat. I shook Dieters hand and thanked him for all his hard work. "It will be reflected in the size of my bill," he replied. I must have looked a bit surprised as all three of them began laughing hysterically, which left me a bit perplexed. "There is no bill," said Dieter, "Nothing to pay at all." "Thank you Dieter," I said. I went to shake Bernd's hand but before I could he thrust an airline ticket into my hand and said, "Time to get back to work David!" "Thanks Bernd," I said, and looked at the ticket. It was for the following day, it was also first class and it also had Ushi's name on it too. Wicked, I'd never flown first class before. "Thanks Bernd," I said again.

Ushi gave me a big cuddle and said, "What do you want to do now?" "Two things," I replied, "The first being let's go to the pub." Not a drop of alcohol had passed my lips for the best part for seven weeks. I was gagging for a pint, followed by another and another and probably another. We retired to the Spandau Brauhaus and proceeded to fulfil my wish..

Lightning Source UK Ltd.
Milton Keynes UK
24 May 2010

154649UK00001B/72/P